CQe

Certified Quality Engineer
Examination Study Guide

by Thomas Pyzdek

The CQE Examination Study Guide

Quality Publishing, Inc.
Tucson, Arizona
1-800-628-0432 FAX 1-800-848-8216

ISBN 0-930011-01-5

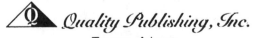 Quality Publishing, Inc.
Tucson, Arizona
1-800-628-0432 FAX 1-800-848-8216

PREFACE

Quality control has existed since mankind first began to create things for his use or enjoyment. But quality is an elusive thing, I have heard the word "quality" defined in many different ways. Each definition has its strengths and weaknesses. Each enjoys its popularity for awhile, some hang on longer than others. Throughout most of history this situation was perfectly satisfactory. Quality, like art, was very much defined by the individual. Today this is no longer good enough, our complex industrial age has forced us to approach quality in a more systematic manner.

One of the results of this is that a body of knowledge has been developed that is, to a considerable extent, unique to the profession of quality control. This body of knowledge is generic, it can be applied to achieve gains at different companies and even in different industries. The accumulation of this body of knowledge began long ago, but it really came into focus with the publication of the book Economic Control of Quality of Manufactured Product by Walter A. Shewhart in 1931. This book literally created the quality control profession. By the end of World War II the techniques used in quality control had become highly developed and specialized. A new group, the Society of

Quality Engineers, was formed to facilitate the exchange of information. The growth continued and the scope of the quality profession expanded, the society became the American Society for Quality Control (ASQC) to reflect this broader mandate. The quality professional had come into his own.

As the years passed it became increasingly clear that there was a need to accredit individuals who had achieved a level of mastery over the body of knowledge that was called "quality control engineering." It was a unique subject matter, unlike that of any other engineering discipline. Employers wanted a credential that denoted recognition of proficiency. Beginning in 1966, ASQC pioneered an important step in professional development. It launched a program of peer recognition for the quality engineer, through formal certification based upon successful attainment of a prescribed combination of education, experience and demonstrated knowledge of the principles and their application within the quality sciences. On June 15, 1968, after a six month "grandfather" period, the first written examinations were conducted for qualified candidates wishing to become ASQC Certified Quality Engineers (CQE). At that time 149 passed the exams, which were held in 15 locations. The program was a success, with many major firms formally endorsing the program and many others giving their tacit endorsement by advertising "ASQC CQE PREFERED." By June 1984 over 10,000 quality professionals had been certified; the June 1984 CQE exam alone was taken by 1,374 candidates at 153 locations in 10 countries!

The exam itself is not easy. It consists of 170 questions covering principles and applications of the subject matter of quality control. It takes six hours to complete. The failure rate historically hovers around 40% to 50%. This has inspired many to prepare for the CQE exam by taking "refresher courses." My experience as an instructor of Quality Engineering is that taking a refresher course improves the chances of success on the CQE exam to over 80%, the effort certainly pays off. However, many people don't have access to such a course. They may live in a remote area, have a job that requires extensive travel, or some other situation prevents them from obtaining this useful training. For them the answer has been self-study. The problem is, just what should be studied? The CQE exam covers a body of knowledge so broad that it takes several years of formal college training just to cover it. Assuming that the prospective CQE wants to review the essential material in 4 to 6 months it becomes imperative that he or she concentrate their efforts on the vital areas.

The CQE Exam: Study Guide was written to help CQE candidates separate the vital information from the vast subject matter covered. It does so by presenting detailed answers to a recently published CQE exam, with frequent references for additional study. It also includes two separate CQE refresher courses based on two fine quality control books, The Quality Control Handbook and Quality Planning and Analysis. The student unable to attend a regularly scheduled refresher course can, in essence, take a refresher course on his own. Quizzes are included to help the student evaluate his progress and a final exam provides a "dress rehearsal" for the real exam. Instructors in CQE refresher courses will also find this book helpful as a supplemental text in their courses.

A note of caution, study of old exams will not prepare you well enough to pass a CQE exam. The questions on the new exam will probably be different than those on the old exams. There is no substitute for a thorough understanding of the subject matter, and this can only be obtained from long and hard study.

TABLE OF CONTENTS

	Page
Introduction	1
Answers to June 1981 CQE Exam	
Principles Portion	6
Applications Portions	62
Appendix	130
Index	175

INTRODUCTION

So, you want to become an ASQC CQE. It won't be easy. The requirements are stringent (see the ASQC booklet "Quality Engineer Certification Program" reprinted in the appendix), and you must pass the CQE exam. The exam consists of 170 questions that cover principles and applications of the body of knowledge known as "quality engineering." It takes six hours to complete the exam. Historically, nearly half of those who qualify and sit for the exam fail it.

However, over **20,000** quality professionals have earned the designation CQE since the program began in 1968. The reasons for doing so vary but they include the satisfaction of peer recognition, the pride of accomplishment, and of course the rewards of the improved job market. Many firms have endorsed the ASQC certification program and the words "ASQC certified prefered" are commonplace in help wanted advertisements. So by all means go for it! The benefits <u>do</u> outweigh the costs.

Once you have decided to take the CQE exam your first step should be to contact ASQC at this address:

> **American Society for Quality Control**
> 611 E Wisconsin Avenue * Milwaukee, WI 53202-4606 * 1-800-952-6587

Tell ASQC that you wish to take the CQE exam and ask them for current literature on membership in ASQC and the

CQE exam. In particular you will want to know the exam schedule, fees, application deadlines, qualifications, and names of local ASQC section officials to contact. You might also ask if there are any section sponsored refresher courses in your area, these courses can dramatically improve your chances for passing the CQE exam.

The CQE exam consists of multiple choice questions that cover eight subject areas. The subject areas, and the approximate percentage of questions (based on exams published in the past) are

- 39% Fundamentals of probability, statistical quality control and design of experiments.
- 15% Metrology, inspection and testing.
- 13% Quality planning, management, and product liability.
- 11% Quality cost analysis.
- 7% Quality information systems.
- 6% Quality auditing.
- 5% Reliability, maintainability, and product safety.
- 4% Human factors and motivation.

Be advised that these percentages are intended as a rough guide only, on any one exam the proportion of questions devoted to a particular subject area can vary considerably. However, the above "pareto analysis" should be useful in planning your study efforts.

A few words of advice on the exam itself. Only certain reference materials are allowed. Usually you are allowed to take in any reference material except materials containing old CQE exam questions or answers. Thus, for example, you are <u>not</u> allowed to use this book as a reference at an exam. I advise that you take the following materials with you as a minimum

* A copy of MIL STD 105 or ANSI/ASQC Z1.4 (Sampling Procedures and Tables for Inspection by Attributes)

* A copy of MIL-STD-414 or ANSI/ASQC Z1.9 (Sampling Procedures and Tables for Inspection by Variables for Percent Nonconforming)

* A good text on fundamental probability and statistics, preferably one you have studied thoroughly

* A good technical and scientific dictionary

* The ASQC publication **"Principles of Quality Costs"**

* The <u>Quality Control Handbook</u>, J.M. Juran, ed.

* A good text on quality control statistics (there are several listed in the bibliography of the ASQC booklet "Quality Engineer Certification Program" which is reprinted in the appendix)

* A calculator that you are familiar with that
computes averages and standard deviations.

Be sure you have fresh batteries!

Exam taking is a rather strenuous physical experience, especially when it takes six hours. Be sure that you
eat regular meals and get adequate sleep for several days
preceeding the exam. This is especially important the day
before the exam. On exam day, eat a moderate breakfast and
lunch, don't starve or stuff yourself. Eat foods that won't
upset your stomach. Don't drink more than one cup of coffee,
studies have shown that more than one cup adversely affects
test taking ability. When taking the exam, do the easiest
questions first. If you get stuck on a question move on
quickly to one you can answer, you can always return to the
tough ones later. Don't be too quick to consult a reference
work, look for an obvious answer first. Before you "guess"
at an answer read the question carefully a second time.
Look for context clues, are several choices ruled out by the
context of the question? Are some choices obviously wrong?
Are there one or more key words in the question that narrow
the choice of answers? Finally, after all other possibilities
have been examined, give it your best guess and move on. Time
management during the exam can be worth several points! Pay
very close attention to the answer sheet, it is machine graded
and you can blow the entire exam by just getting off one space.

Finally, be aware that you will never pass the CQE exam if you rely solely on old exams for study. This book is merely a study guide, not a comprehensive reference. If you are serious about the CQE exam you must spend a great deal of time burning the midnight oil studying the references cited. Take a refresher course or, if this isn't possible, take one of the 15 week courses outlined in the appendix on a self-study basis. Many organizations, including ASQC, offer short seminars on quality engineering that provide an excellent review of the subject matter. It isn't easy to attain the status of ASQC Certified Quality Engineer, but its worth the effort. Good luck!

Annotated answers to the ASQC CQE exam given in June 1981 and published in the July 1984 Quality Progress magazine.

PRINCIPLES

1. A null hypothesis assumes that a process is producing no more than the maximum allowable rate of defective items. The type II error is to conclude that the process

   1. is producing too many defectives when it actually isn't.

   2. is not producing too many defectives when it actually is.

   3. is not producing too many defectives when it is not.

   4. is producing too many defectives when it is.

The Type II error is the probability that a hypothesis that is false will be accepted. The null hypothesis will be false when the process is producing too many defectives. Thus the correct answer is 2.

2. A number derived from sample data, which describes the data in some useful way, is called a

   1. constant.

   2. statistic.

   3. parameter.

   4. critical value.

A <u>STATISTIC</u> is a value computed from <u>SAMPLE DATA</u>. Statistics are often used to make inferences about POPULATION PARAMETERS. The correct answer is 2.

    3. The spread of individual observations from a normal process capability distribution may be expressed numerically as

    1. $6\overline{R}/d_2$

    2. $2 \times A_2 \overline{R}$

    3. $\overline{R}/d_2$

    4. $D_4\overline{R}$

If and only if a process is in control then the standard deviation can be estimated from the average range by the equation $s = \overline{R}/d_2$ where s = Standard deviation

               $\overline{R}$ = The average range

               d_2 = A table factor that depends on the sample size.

In quality control we often estimate the capability of a normally distributed process to be 6s, as illustrated below.

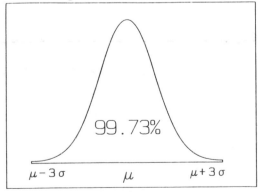

Thus the correct answer is 1.

4. In MIL-STD-105D, the AQL is always determined at

what P_a on the OC curve?

1. 0.05

2. 0.10

3. 0.90

4. 0.95

5. None of the above.

With MIL-STD-105D the probability of acceptance (P_a) given an AQL (Acceptable Quality Level) process varies. ·The answer is 5.

5. For the Normal Probability Distribution, the relation-

ships among the median, mean and mode are that

1. they are all equal to the same value.

2. the mean and mode have the same value but the

median is different.

3. each has a value different from the other two.

4. the mean and median are ths same but the mode is

different.

The normal distribution is unimodal and symmetric; thus the mean, median, and mode are all the same (answer #1).

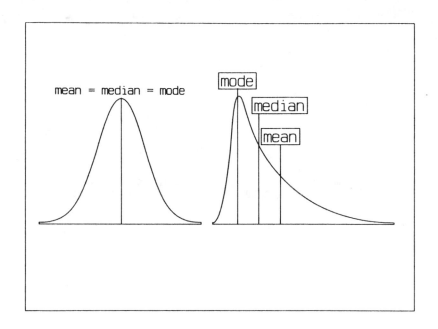

Definitions

Mean   = Sum of values/Number of values.

Median = Value that 50% are greater than and
         50% are less than.

Mode   = The value that occurs most frequently.

6. The test used for testing significance in an Analysis
   of Variance table
   1. the z test.
   2. the t test.
   3. the F test.
   4. the Chi-square test.

The F test is used to test the hypothesis that two sample
variances are equal. This is correct for the Analysis of
Variance (ANOVA) since we compare the within group variance
to the between group variances. Choice 3 is correct.
(Note: ANOVA is a test of the equality of _means_, not
variances.)

7. A sample of n observations has a mean $\overline{X}$ and standard deviation $s_x > 0$. If a single observation, which equals the value of the sample mean $\overline{X}$, is removed from the sample, which of the following is true?

1. $\overline{X}$ and s_x both change.

2. $\overline{X}$ and s_x remain the same.

3. $\overline{X}$ remains the same but s_x increases.

4. $\overline{X}$ remains the same but s_x decreases.

The two equations of interest are

$$\overline{X} = \frac{1}{n} \sum_{i=1}^{n} Xi \qquad \text{and} \qquad S = \frac{\sum_{i=1}^{n} (Xi - \overline{X})^2}{n - 1}$$

Since S>0 we know that $Xi \neq \overline{X}$ for at least one i. If we remove a single observation exactly equal to $\overline{X}$ then the numerator sum in the equation of S will be unchanged (since we are deleting a zero) but the denominator will change from n-1 to n-2; thus S will increase. The next task is to show that $\overline{X}$ will be unchanged. Let us define

$$S1 = \sum_{i=1}^{n} Xi \qquad \text{and} \qquad S2 = S1 - \overline{X}$$

The value of $\overline{X}$ after removing a value exactly equal to $\overline{X}$ will be

$$\overline{X}_2 = S2/(n-1) = \frac{S1 - \overline{X}}{n-1} = \frac{S1 - \frac{S1}{n}}{n-1} = \frac{S1(\frac{n-1}{n})}{n-1} = S1/n = \overline{X}$$

Q.E.D.

The correct answer is 3.

8. The Dodge-Romig Tables are designed to minimize

   which parameter?

   1. AOQL

   2. AQL

   3. ATI

   4. AOQ

Dodge-Romig tables contain single and double acceptance sampling plans that minimize the Average Total Inspected (ATI) subject to a constrained Average Outgoing Quality Limit (AOQL) or Lot Tolerance Percent Defective (LTPD). The correct choice is 3.

9. In a single factor analysis of variance, the

   assumption of homogeneity of variances applies to

   1. the variances within the treatment groups.

   2. the variance of the treatment means.

   3. the total variance.

   4. All of the above.

In single factor (or any other) analysis of variance we assume the <u>within group</u> variance is homogeneous, i.e. it doesn't change from group to group. This assumption is vital to the validity of the tests of hypotheses. Statistical tests exist to check this assumption.

10. When used together for variables data, which of the following pair of quantities is the most useful in preparing control charts?

1. AQL, p'

2. p, n

3. $\overline{X}$, R

4. R, σ

The best choice is 3. Choices 1 and 2 refer to attributes data quality measures. Both the values in choice 4 refer to measures of <u>dispersion</u>. Only choice 3 can measure both central tendency and dispersion for a process.

11. An operation requires shipments from your vendor of small lots of fixed size. The attribute sampling plan used for receiving inspection should have its OC curve developed using

1. the Binomial distribution.

2. the Gaussian (normal) distribution.

3. the Poisson distribution.

4. the Hypergeometric distribution.

Since the question refers to attribute sampling we can rule out choice 2, which applies to variables data. Choices 1 and 3 assume large lots. The hypergeometric distribution is the correct choice for small isolated lots and attribute inspection.

12. The acronym "AQL," as used in sampling inspection, means

    1. that level of lot quality for which there is a small risk of rejecting the lot.

    2. the Average Quality Limit.

    3. the maximum percent defective that can be considered satisfactory as a process average.

    4. the quality level.

The term AQL, or acceptable quality level, is defined in Military Standard 105D as

> "the maximum percent defective (or defects per hundred units) that, for purposes of sampling inspection, can be considered satisfactory as a process average."

Thus #3 is correct.

13. A 3^2 experiment means that we are considering

    1. two levels of three factors.

    2. two dependent variables and three independent variables.

    3. two go/no-go variables and three continuous variables.

    4. three levels of two factors.

Standard notation for designed experiments where there are n factors all at L levels is L^n. Thus choice 4 is correct.

14. An operating characteristic curve shows

    1. the probability of accepting lots of various
       quality levels by sampling methods.

    2. the operating characteristics of a machine.

    3. how to operate a machine for best quality results.

    4. the probability that a lot contains a certain
       number of rejectable parts.

A typical operating characteristics curve (OC curve) is shown below. The vertical axis shows the probability of accepting the null hypothesis using a sampling scheme, the horizontal axis shows the actual "state of nature." In a typical quality control application the state of nature would be the process quality levels. This makes choice 1 the best.

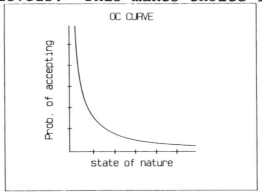

15. Basic assumptions underlying the Analysis of Variance
    include

    A. observations are from normally distributed
       populations.

    B. observations are from populations with equal
       variances.

    C. observations are from populations with equal means.

1. A and B only

2. A and C only

3. B and C only

4. A, B and C

Choices A and B are the basic assumptions. Choice C is the null hypothesis we usually test with ANOVA. Thus choice 1 is best.

16. Two quanitities which uniquely determine a single sampling attributes plan are

1. AQL and LTPD.

2. sample size and rejection number.

3. AQL and producer's risk.

4. LTPD and consumer's risk.

The sample size and rejection number uniquely determine a single attributes sampling plan. All of the other choices are operating characteristics.

17. All of the following statements are true **except**

1. in multiple regression, extrapolation beyond the region of observations can lead to erroneous predications.

2. at least 3 variables are involved in multiple regression.

3. multiple regression involves one independent and two or more dependent variables.

16

The multiple regression model has one <u>dependent</u> variable and
two or more <u>independent</u> variables. For example, a multiple
linear regression model might be

$$Y = B_0 + B_1X_1 + B_2X_2$$

where Y = The dependent variable

X_1 and X_2 = Independent variables

Thus choice 3 is not incorrect.

<u>Extrapolation</u> beyond the region of observation is always
risky. Here is an example

Based on this model we might project a 25 year old to be
over 9 feet tall!

18. The primary advantage of the Latin Square design,

compared to the factorial design, is that

1. it requires less data.

2. it eliminates the need for interaction analysis.

3. it allows higher significance levels.

4. it does not require homogeneity of variance.

The factorial design provides a means of testing for <u>interaction</u> effects, while the Latin Square does not. The additional information requires additional data for factorial designs, making choice 1 correct. Latin Square designs do not "eliminate the need for interaction analysis," they do, however, assume that interaction effects are negligible.

19. For two events, A and B, one of the following is a true probability statement.

1. P(A or B) = P(A) + P(B) if A and B are independent.

2. P(A or B) = P(A) + P(B) if A and B are mutually exclusive.

3. P(A and B) = P(A) × P(B) if A and B are mutually exclusive.

4. P(A and B) = P(A) × P(B) if A and B are independent.

Choice 2 is correct, as is easily seen from the Venn diagram below

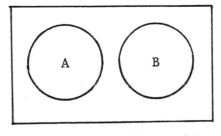

Sample space

P(A or B) = P(A) + P(B)

Two events A and B are mutually exclusive if they have no common elements. That is, the <u>intersection</u> of A and B is is an empty set.

20. Which one of the following BEST describes machine capability?

    1. The total variation of all cavities of a mold, cavities of a die cast machine or spindles of an automatic assembly machine.

    2. The inherent variation of the machine.

    3. The total variation over a shift.

    4. The variation in a short run of consecutively produced parts.

Choice 2 is best. Inherent variability is the variation that remains after all assignable causes of variation have been eliminated. It is often called random variation.

21. In comparison with attributes sampling plans, variables sampling plans

    1. have the advantage of greater simplicity.

    2. usually require a larger sample size for comparable assurance as to the correctness of decisions in judging a single quality characteristic.

    3. have the advantage of being applicable to either single or multiple quality characteristics.

    4. provide greater assurance, for the same sample size, as to the correctness of decisions in judging a single quality characteristic.

Choice 4 is correct. The converse is also true; that is, for a given level of assurance a variables sampling plan requires a smaller sample size.

22. To state that a model in an experimental design is fixed indicates that

1. the levels used for each factor are the only ones of interest.

2. the levels were chosen from a fixed population.

3. the equipment from which the data are collected must not be moved.

4. the factors under consideration are qualitative.

There are two types of factors in any experiment, fixed and random. A fixed factor is one where all levels of interest of the factor are chosen. For example, if the experiment involves a 4 spindle drill and all four spindles are considered. A random factor is one where only a sample of all possible levels are tried. An example would be an experiment that gathers data from 5 machines when the intent is to extrapolate the results to 10 other machines. Choice 1 is correct.

23. Which of the following cannot be a null hypothesis?

1. The population means are equal.

2. $p' = 0.5$

3. The sample means are equal.

4. The difference in the population means is 3.85

Null hypotheses refer to <u>populations</u>, not samples (see question #14 in this section for an example). Thus choice 3 can not be a null hypothesis.

24. You have been doing precision testing on a special

order micrometer delivered by a vendor. The sample

size in your test was 25 readings. The acceptance

specification requires a precision sigma of .003 inch.

Your observed precision sigma was .0033 inch. Although

the observed precision did not meet the requirements,

you are reluctant to reject it because you need it

badly. You should

1. accept it because it is close enough.

2. reject it because it did not meet the criteria.

3. apply the Chi-square test to see if the micrometer

should be accepted.

4. apply the F test to see if the micrometer should

be accepted.

5. send the micrometer to the gage lab for adjustment.

The correct statistical test to apply when testing the hypothesis that a population standard deviation is less than or equal to a "target" standard deviation is the Chi-square test. The null hypothesis is

$$H : \sigma = \sigma_0$$

where σ = The population standard deviation

σ_0 = The target standard deviation

for our case here σ_0 = .003. The test statistic

$$\chi^2 = \frac{(n-1)\ s^2}{\sigma_0{}^2} = \frac{24\ (.0033)^2}{(.003)^2}$$

has a Chi-square distribution with 24 degrees of freedom. Choice 3 is correct.

25. If, in a t-test, alpha is .05,

   1. 5% of the time we will say that there is no real

      difference, but in reality there is a difference.

   2. 5% of the time we will make a correct inference.

   3. 5% of the time we will say that there is a real

      difference when there really is not a difference.

   4. 95% of the time we will make an incorrect inference.

   5. 95% of the time the null hypothesis will be correct.

Alpha, also known as Type I error or level of significance, is the probability of rejecting the null hypothesis when it is actually true. In a t test we are testing a hypothesis regarding the equality of two means based on samples, namely,

$$H : \mu_1 = \mu_2$$

If α = .05 then we will reject the null hypothesis (i.e. say there is a difference) when in fact the null hypothesis is true (i.e. there is no difference) 5% of the time. This is choice 3.

26. The expression $P(x) = \dfrac{u^x \cdot e^{-u}}{x!}$ is the general term for the

    1. Poisson Distribution.

    2. Pascal Distribution

    3. Hypergeometric Distribution.

    4. Binomial Distribution.

The expression is the probability density function of the Poisson Distriubtion, choice 1. In a typical quality control application u would be the average rate of defects-per-unit and x would be the defect count. With this sort of question you must read the question with extreme care, previous exams have had equations that differ from a well known distribution in only a very small (but vital) detail.

27. An experiment with two factors, in which all levels of one variable are run at each level of the second variable, is called a

    1. one-way experiment.

    2. Latin square experiment.

    3. factorial experiment.

    4. fractional factorial experiment.

The answer is #3. These experiments are sometimes called full factorial experiments to distinguish them from fractional factorial experiments. A fractional factorial experiment is one where only some of the possible factor combinations are tried, an example is shown below.

Fractional Factorial Experiment

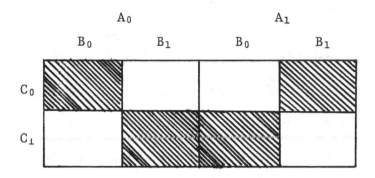

This is a half fraction of a three factor experiment, each factor at 2 levels. Standard notation: 2^{3-1} experiment.

28. How many outcomes are possible when performing a single trial of a binomial experiment?

1. One

2. Two

3. Three

By definition, there are two possible outcomes from a single trial of a binomial experiment, choice 2. A typical quality control example would be an inspection of a unit where the unit is to be classified as either conforming or non-conforming.

29. Under acceptance sampling, with screening, average outgoing quality will not be worse, in the long run, than the

1. ATI

2. AQL

3. AOQL

4. AOQ

When acceptance sampling is performed and rejected lots are 100% inspected, with defectives removed or replaced with non-defectives, the average outgoing quality (AOQ) is related to the incoming quality. There is a maximum average outgoing quality for all possible incoming quality levels, known as the average outgoing quality limit or AOQL. This is choice 3.

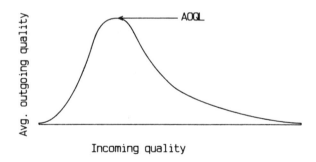

30. Which of the following does not generate product-quality characteristics?

1. Designer.

2. Inspector.

3. Machinist.

4. Equipment engineer.

Inspectors do not <u>generate</u> quality characteristics; they merely compare them to operational standards. Choice 2 is correct.

31. A comparison of variable and attribute sampling systems will show that equal protection (as determined by the OC curves) can be obtained

1. when the variable and attribute sample size are equal.

2. when the attribute sample is smaller than the variable sample.

3. when the variable sample is smaller than the attribute sample.

4. None of these.

Choice 3 is correct. Also see #21 of this section.

32. A quality control program is considered to be

1. a collection of quality control procedures and guidelines.

2. a step by step list of all quality control check points.

3. a summary of company quality control policies.

4. a system of activities to provide quality of products and service.

A quality control program is more than just procedures, lists, or policy summaries. It is the system of all activities that provide quality products and services. Choice 4 is best.

33. A milestone in product liability was accomplished
    in 1963 as a result of "Greenman vs. Yuba Power
    Products Inc." The court stated that, "The costs
    of injuries resulting from defective products are
    borne by the manufacturers that put such products
    on the market, rather than by the injured persons
    who are powerless to protect themselves." This
    ruling caused a phase-out of which of the following
    concepts?

    1. Implied warranty.

    2. Caveat emptor.

    3. Privity of contract.

    4. Res ipsa loquitur.

In contract law, privity denotes parties in mutual legal
relationship to each other by virtue of being promisees and
promisors. At early common law, third-party assignees were
said to be not in "privity." Thus, the manufacturers were
held not liable for defective product they purchased from
vendors or sold to a consumer through a chain of wholesalers,
dealers, etc. This concept began to deteriorate in 1905 when
courts began to permit lawsuits against sellers of unwhole-
some food, whether or not they were negligent, and against
original manufacturers, whether or not they were in privity
with the consumers. The first recognition of strict liability for an express warranty without regard to privity was

enunciated by a Washington court in 1932 in a case involving a Ford Motor Company express warranty that their windshields were "shatterproof." When the windshield shattered and injured a consumer the court allowed the suit against Ford, ruling that even without privity the manufacturer was responsible for the misrepresentation, even if the misrepresentation was done innocently.

Under the rule of STRICT LIABILITY an innocent consumer who knows nothing about disclaimers and the requirement of giving notice to a manufacturer with whom he did not deal cannot be prevented from suing. The rule avoids the technical limits of privity, which can create a chain of lawsuits back to the party that originally put the defective product into the stream of commerce. The seller (whether a salesman or manufacturer) is liable even though he has been careful in handling the product and even if the consumer did not deal directly with him.

The first case to apply this modern rule was Greenman vs. Yuba Power Products, Inc. in California in 1963. A party, Mr. Greenman, was injured when a workpiece flew from a combination power tool purchased for him by his wife two years prior to the injury. He sued the manufacturer and produced witnesses to prove that the machine was designed with inadequate set screws.

The manufacturer, who had advertised the power tool as having "rugged construction" and "positive locks that hold through rough or precision work" claimed that it should not have to pay money damages because the plaintiff had not given it notice of breach of warranty within a reasonable time as required. Furthermore, a long line of California cases had held that a plaintiff could not sue someone not in privity with him unless the defective product was food.

The court replied that this was not a warranty case but a STRICT LIABILITY case. The decision stated that any "manufacturer is strictly liable . . . when an article he placed on the market, knowing that it is to be used without inspection for defects, proves to have a defect that causes injury to a human being."

The fundamental concepts of product liability are covered very well in

> The Reader's Digest Family Legal Guide, Dobelis, I.N., ed., West Publishing Company, Pleasantville, NY, 1981, pages 765-773.

34. When planning a total quality system, one key objective is to provide a means of guaranteeing "the maintenance of product integrity." Which of the following quality system provisions is designed to MOST directly provide such a guarantee?

1. Drawing and print control.

2. Calibration and maintenance of test equipment.

3. Identification and segregation of non-conforming material.

4. Specification change control.

The key words here are <u>MOST</u> <u>DIRECT</u>. While all of the choices provide a means of guaranteeing the maintenance of product integrity, identification and segregation of non-conforming material, choice 3, is the most direct means.

35. The primary reason for evaluating and maintaining surveillance over a supplier's quality program is to

   1. perform product inspection at source.

   2. eliminate incoming inspection cost.

   3. motivate suppliers to improve quality.

   4. make sure the supplier's quality program is functioning effectively.

While all choices are valid reasons for evaluating and maintaining surveillance over a supplier's quality program, choice 4 is the <u>primary</u> reason.

36. The primary reason for first-piece inspection is to

   1. approve a set up for further production.

   2. accept a lot prior to completion of the lot.

   3. try out a new inspection method.

   4. eliminate need for further inspection.

Choice 1 is the only valid reason given for first-piece inspection.

37. Machine capability studies on four machines yielded the following information:

Machine	Average ($\overline{X}$)	Capability(6σ)
#1	1.495	.004"
#2	1.502	.006"
#3	1.500	.012"
#4	1.498	.012"

The tolerance on the particular dimension is 1.500±
.005". If the average value can be readily shifted
by adjustment to the machine, then the BEST machine
to use is

1. Machine #1.

2. Machine #2.

3. Machine #3.

4. Machine #4.

Since we can, by assumption, shift the average value, the $\overline{X}$
column can be ignored. Thus the best choice is the machine
with the least dispersion, which is machine #1.

38. Based on the information given in the above question,
    if the average value cannot be readily shifted by
    adjustment to the machine and no rework or repair
    is possible, then the BEST machine to use is

    1. Machine #1.

    2. Machine #2.

    3. Machine #3.

    4. Machine #4.

We now seek the machine which gives the smallest proportion discrepant. If we assume a normal distribution for each machine, the answer will be found using the Z statistics for each machine, namely

$$Z = \frac{spec - \overline{X}}{\sigma}$$

This gives

Machine	$Z_{low\ spec}$	$Z_{high\ spec}$
#1	0	+15.0
#2	-7.0	+3.0
#3	-2.5	+2.5
#4	-1.5	+3.5

A casual glance through the normal tables (which is all you'll have time for in the real CQE exam) will show that machine #2 is easily the best choice.

39. Incoming-material inspection is based most directly on

1. design requirements.

2. purchase order requirements.

3. manufacturing requirements.

4. customer use of the end product.

Again the key words are <u>most</u> <u>directly</u>, and choice 2 is the best.

40. The "quality function" of a company is best described as

1. the degree to which the company product conforms to a design or specification.

2. that collection of activities through which "fitness for use" is achieved.

3. the degree to which a class or category of product possesses satisfaction for people generally.

4. All of the above.

The "quality function" is analagous to the "quality program" discussed in question 32. The best choice is #2.

41. The advantage of a written procedure is

1. it provides flexibility in dealing with problems.

2. unusual conditions are handled better.

3. it is a perpetual coordination device.

4. coordination with other departments is not required.

The <u>only</u> valid choice is #3. None of the others are advantages of written procedures, in fact they are among the <u>disadvantages</u> of written procedures!

42. In spite of the Quality Engineer's best efforts, situations may develop in which his decision is overruled. The most appropriate action would be to

1. resign his position based upon his convictions.

2. report his findings to an outside source such as a regulatory agency or the press.

3. document his findings, report to his superiors, and move on to the next assignment.

   4. discuss his findings with his co-workers in order

      to gain support, thereby forcing action.

The "correct" answer to this question depends on the circumstances. In matters of safety and health threats you are at times morally _and_ _legally_ obligated to take the actions described by choices 1 or 2. However, in the vast majority of cases choice 3 is best.

   43. In preparing a Product Quality Policy for your

       company, you should do all of the following **except**

       1. specify the means by which quality performance

          is measured.

       2. develop criteria for identifying risk situations

          and specify whose approval is required when there

          are known risks.

       3. include procedural matters and functional

          responsibilities.

       4. state quality goals.

Choice 3 is not appropriate material for a quality _policy_.

   44. Which of the following is most important when

       calibrating a piece of equipment?

       1. Calibration sticker.

       2. Maintenance history card.

       3. Standard used.

       4. Calibration interval.

If the calibration standard is inadequate the other 3 items
are meaningless. Choice 3 is correct.

45. A "negative" specification on an attribute (such as
    Salmonella) of a food product generally means
    1. that gram negative organisms are permissible.
    2. that given the state of the technology, none can
       be detected.
    3. that levels above one part per billion are to be
       rejected.
    4. None of the above.

Choice 2 is the definition of a negative specification in the
food industry.

46. Products should be subjected to tests which are
    designed to
    1. demonstrate advertised performance.
    2. demonstrate basic function at minimum testing cost.
    3. approximate the conditions to be experienced in
       customer's application.
    4. assure that specifications are met under laboratory
       conditions.
    5. assure performance under severe environmental
       conditions.

Under the "fitness for use" definition of quality, choice 3
is the best. Keep in mind that if a different context were

presented one of the other choices might be better (e.g.
choice 5 might be best for a prototype guided missile).

47. Holography is a non-destructive test technique which

    is used to

    1. measure hole locations with an optical device.

    2. measure the depth of "halos" around drilled

       holes using X-ray.

    3. measure the continuity of plated-through holes

       in printed wiring boards.

    4. measure surface displacements by recording

       interference patterns.

    5. measure flaws using acoustic vibration.

Holography is a system of recording light or other waves on a
photographic plate or other medium in such a way as to allow
a three-dimensional reconstruction of the scene giving rise
to the waves. The plate, or hologram, records the inter-
ference pattern between waves reflected by the scene and a
direct reference wave at an angle to it. Choice 4 is the
correct one.

48. Characteristics for which 100% inspection may be

    practicable include all of the following **except**

    1. dimensions subject to measurements or go/no-go gaging.

    2. performance characteristics subject to non-

       destructive testing.

3. characteristics observable by visual inspection.

4. ultimate physical properties (tensile strength, viscosity).

Choice 4 includes destructive tests, for which 100% inspection is clearly inappropriate.

49. The strength of a magnetic field is known as

1. flux density.

2. ferromagnetic force.

3. magnetic polarity.

4. coercive force.

The strength of a magnetic field is known as the flux density, choice 1. The unit of flux in SI units is the Weber (Wb), defined such that an electromotive force of one volt is induced in a single coil when the flux changes in the coil at the rate of one Wb per second.

50. In the drawing tolerance

⊕	0.005	Ⓜ	A	B	C

, C is the

1. primary datum.

2. tertiary datum.

3. basic datum.

4. largest datum.

ANSI Y14.5M-1982 Section 4.3 states

"To properly position a part on the datum

reference frame, datums must be specified

in an order of preference."

The datum reference frame described involves three mutually

perpendicular datum planes. <u>Datum features</u> which are to be

used to establish these datum planes are shown in the <u>feature</u>

<u>control block</u> in order of precedence, as shown below

<u>FEATURE CONTROL BLOCK</u>

Thus choice 2 is correct.

51. Station control is

    1. a technique to implement quality plans in the shop.

    2. applied to assure that planned quality performance

       is consistently and economically maintained.

    3. a technique which emphasizes control of input.

    4. All of the above.

The concept of station control is described in

Quality Control Handbook, Third Edition,
J.M. Juran, ed., pp. 9-43, 9-44, McGraw Hill,
New York, 1974.

The building blocks of manufacturing processes are "operations," i.e., the elemental processes which bring about some intended change in the characteristics of the product. These operations are grouped into "work stations." As the concept of quality control has evolved, it has deemphasized product inspection and has looked to process design and control as the prime source of quality. The control criteria includes such things as

- Product criteria
- Process operation criteria
- Process control criteria
- Machine and tool maintenance criteria
- Instrument maintenance criteria
- Responsibilities on the factory floor

Obviously, choice 4 is correct.

52. A tracer type surface finish instrument, such as a profilometer, can be used to measure all of the following **except**

1. roughness on gear teeth.
2. depth of scratches on a metal surface.
3. roughness on mild steel plate.
4. surface quality of a tapered hole.

Surface finish involves a number of characteristics and concepts

- "Roughness", which describes the fine

regularly-spaced asperities caused by cutting tools, grinding wheels, or polishing machines.

- "Waviness" denotes more widely spaced repetitive features which result from machine vibration, tool chatter, work-piece deflection or warping of the material itself.

- "Lay" is the term given to the predominant direction of the pattern formed by regular surface features. Lay is determined by the production process.

- "Flaws" are random imperfections such as voids, scratches, digs, holes, inclusions, etc.

Surface finish, as measured with traces type surface finish instruments, are measured perpendicular to the lay and do not include random flaws. Thus choice 2 is correct. Interested readers can find an excellent series of articles entitled "A Surface View", Quality Magazine, June 1982 (pp. 16-23) and September 1982 (pp. 26-31).

53. Which material listed below can be usefully tested by the magnetic particle method?

1. Carbon steel

2. Aluminum

3. Magnesium

4. Lead

5. None of the above.

Magnetic particle inspection only works with ferromagnetic materials. Of the four choices, only carbon steel, choice 1, is ferromagnetic.

54. Where inspector efficiency is defined as the ratio of correct decisions to the total decisions regarding individual items, most inspection operations performed by human inspectors are approximately

1. 40 - 55% efficient.

2. 55 - 70% efficient.

3. 70 - 95% efficient.

4. 95 - 100% efficient.

Emperical studies repeatedly show that inspector accuracy falls in the range given by choice 3 - 70% to 95%. One such study is

Wang, S.C., "Human Reliability In Visual Inspection," Quality, Sept. 1975, pp. 24-25.

55. Terminal based linearity, as applied to the linearity accuracy of voltage or resistance division of slide wires, potentiometers, stepdividers, etc., is defined as

1. the maximum deviation from an arc of 180°, based on the effective electrical travel.

2. the maximum deviation from a straight line which passes through the zero and 100 percent points, based on the effective electrical travel.

3. the algebraic difference of the end-scale values.

4. the percent of the end-scale value of an instrument that corresponds to the end-scale indication.

5. None of the above.

According to the Van Nostrand Scientific Encyclopedia (Litton Educational Publishing, Inc. 1976), Terminal based linearity is "the maximum deviation of the actual characteristic (average of upscale and downscale readings) from a straight line coinciding with the actual characteristic at upper and lower range values." Choice 2.

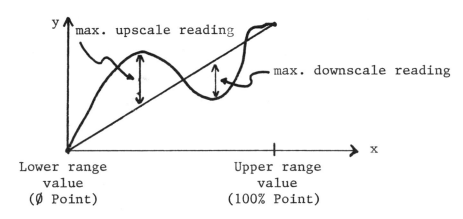

56. Why would inspection by variables be superior to inspection by attributes?

A. Inspection by variables is easier to administer than inspection by attributes.

B. More information is obtained when inspection by variables is utilized.

C. Inspection by variables usually requires smaller samples than inspection by attributes.

1. B only

2. C only

3. A and B only

4. A, B and C

The "official" answer is choice 1, B only. "B" is certainly true since variables data provides information about centering, spread, distribution shape, outliers, etc. that are not provided by attributes data. However, since variables plans provide protection equal to attributes plans with smaller sample sizes (see questions 21 and 31), one could argue in favor of choice 2 (C only). My personal opinion is that "B and C only" would be the best, but this choice isn't offered.

57. In life cycle costing, the term "life" refers to whose viewpoint?

1. Producer's.

2. User's.

3. Contractor's.

4. Quality control.

Life cycle cost concepts are based on the user's perspective; choice 2 is best. Life cycle cost takes into account purchase price, maintenance costs, resale value, etc.

58. Which of the following quality cost indices is likely to have the greatest appeal to top management as an indicator of relative cost?

1. Quality cost per unit of product.

2. Quality cost per hour of direct production labor.

3. Quality cost per unit of processing cost.

4. Quality cost per unit of sales.

5. Quality cost per dollar of direct production labor.

Top management is more accustomed to viewing most costs relative to sales than any of the other indices given. Thus choice 4 is best. However, other company groups (engineering, manufacturing, etc.) may find the costs relative to one of the other indices more useful.

*   *   *

Notes on Quality Costs

This exam, and most previous exams, has a number of questions relating to quality costs. The recommended guidelines for quality cost accounting is described in

> "Quality Costs - What and How", 2nd ed., prepared
> by Quality Cost - Cost Effectiveness Technical
> Committee, ASQC, 1971. 54 pages.

If you plan to take the CQE exam you should obtain this reference. For our purposes here the following definitions are provided (Quality Planning and Analysis, 2nd ed., Juran and Gryna):

Internal Failure Costs: Costs that would disappear if no defects existed prior to shipment to the customer. Examples: scrap, rework, retest, downtime, yield losses, etc.

External Failure Costs: Costs for defects found after shipment to the customer. Examples: complaint adjustment, returned material, warranty, and allowances.

Appraisal Costs: Costs incurred to discover the condition of the product during the "first time through." Examples: incoming material inspection, inprocess inspection and test, calibration, etc.

Prevention Costs: Costs incurred to keep appraisal and failure costs to a minimum. Examples: quality planning, design review, quality training, new-product planning, process control; quality data acquisition, analysis, and reporting; quality improvement projects, etc.

*   *   *

59. Review of purchase orders for quality requirements falls into which one of the following quality cost segments?

1. Prevention.

2. Appraisal.

3. Internal failures.

4. External failures.

Purchase order review is performed to reduce appraisal and failure costs, thus it is a prevention cost, choice 1.

60. Failure costs include costs due to

1. quality control engineering.

2. inspection set-up for tests.

3. certification of special-process suppliers.

4. supplier analysis of non-conforming hardware.

The choices can be categorized as follows:

Choice 1: Prevention.

Choice 2: Appraisal.

Choice 3: Prevention.

Choice 4: Failure.

61. Quality cost trend analysis is facilitated by com-

paring quality costs to

1. manufacturing costs over the same time period.

2. cash flow reports.

3. appropriate measurement bases.

4. QC department budget.

As discussed in question 58, the appropriate measurement base varies with the cost category and the audience. Therefore choice 3 is best.

62. Which of the following is least likely to be

reported as a failure-related cost?

1. Sorting lots rejected by a sampling procedure.

2. Downtime caused by late delivery of a purchased

part rejected by the supplier's final inspection.

3. Repair of field failures.

4. Retesting of a repaired product.

While all of the costs shown are failure costs, common sense would indicate that choice 2 is LEAST LIKELY TO BE REPORTED as a failure related cost.

63. The basic objective of a quality cost program is to

    1. identify the source of quality failures.

    2. interface with the accounting department.

    3. improve the profit of your company.

    4. identify quality control department costs.

The basic objective of a quality cost program is profit improvement, choice 3. A discussion of the relationship of quality costs and profits is given in

    Pyzdek, T., "The Impact of Quality Cost Reduction on Profits," Quality Progress, Oct. 1976.

64. Cost of calibrating test and inspection equipment would be included in

    1. prevention cost.

    2. appraisal cost.

    3. failure cost.

    4. material-procurement cost.

Our cost category definitions clearly place these costs in the appraisal category, choice 2.

65. In some instances, the ordinary cost-balance formula is not valid and cannot be applied because of the

presence of vital intangibles. Such an intangible

involves

1. safety of human beings.

2. compliance with legislation.

3. apparatus for collection of revenue.

4. credit to marketing as new sales for warranty

   replacements.

5. None of the above.

When human safety is at issue the analysis must extend beyond
cost-benefit relationships and include, among other things,
discussion of moral, ethical, and legal aspects of any
decision. Choice 1 is correct.

66. When looking for existing sources of external failure

   cost data, which of the following is usually the best

   source available?

   1. Customer corrective action requests.

   2. Salesmen's field reports.

   3. Accounting reports on "sales of seconds" or

      "distressed merchandise."

   4. Returned material reports.

Based on my experience, I concur that the best source of
external failure cost data (of the choices given) are
returned material reports, choice 4. However, I have found

that excellent data usually exists on total warranty, including returned goods, field repair, etc.

67. The quality assurance function is comparable to
which of the following other business functions
in concept?

    1. General accounting.

    2. Cost accounting.

    3. Audit accounting.

    4. All of the above.

Quality assurance and audit accounting have several similarities. In both activities we seek independent verification by qualified auditors that an adequate system exists and is being followed. Choice 3 is correct.

68. The term "quality audit" can refer to the
appraisal of the quality system of

    1. an entire plant or company.

    2. one product.

    3. one major quality activity.

    4. Any of the above.

The term quality audit is used in a very broad sense, choice 4 is correct.

69. You would normally NOT include data from which
of the following investigations in quality auditing?

1. Examination of all items produced.

2. Examination of customer needs and the adequacy
   of design specifications in reflecting these needs.

3. Examination of vendor product specifications and
   monitoring procedures.

4. Examination of customer quality complaints and
   adequacy of corrective action.

The purpose of an audit is to assure that an effective system
has been developed and is being followed. Choice 1 does not
fit this purpose.

70. In order to be effective, the Quality Audit function
    should ideally be

    1. an independent organizational segment in the
       Quality Control function.

    2. an independent organizational segment in the
       Production Control function.

    3. an independent organizational segment in
       Manufacturing operations function.

    4. All of the above.

The objectivity of the audit function is better assured by
having the function report independently of the groups being
audited. Choice 1 provides this objectivity.

71. Which of the following quality system provisions
    is of the greatest concern when preparing an audit

check list for a quality system audit?

1. Drawing and print control.

2. Make-up of the MRB (Material Review Board).

3. Training level of inspectors.

4. Optimization of production processes.

5. Calibration of test equipment.

The official answer is choice 5; it may be argued that the other choices are not really quality systems per se.

72. The following are reasons why an independent audit of actual practice versus procedures should be performed periodically.

A. Pressures may force the supervisor to deviate from approved procedures.

B. The supervisor may not have time for organized follow-up or adherence to procedures.

C. Supervisors are not responsible for implementing procedures.

1. A and B only

2. B and C only

3. A and C only

4. A, B and C

The best choice is 1, A and B only. All other choices are incorrect since they include C and C is not true.

73. A Vendor Quality Survey

    1. is used to predict whether a potential vendor can meet quality requirements.

    2. is an audit of a vendor's product for a designated period of time.

    3. is always conducted by Quality Control personnel only.

    4. reduces cost by eliminating the need for receiving inspection of the surveyed vendor's product.

The correct answer is choice 1. Just how accurate this prediction is has been debated for many years. Choices 2, 3, and 4 are often untrue.

74. The greatest contribution of a reliability effort is made in the

    1. design area.

    2. manufacturing area.

    3. shipping area.

    4. field service area.

The contribution of the design function to product reliability is unquestionably the greatest; choice 1.

75. Preliminary hazard analysis

    1. is a review of safety problems prior to production.

    2. is normally done at a time when there is little

design detail.

3. can be used to identify the principal hazards
   when the product is first conceived.

4. All of the above.

Preliminary hazard analysis is a review of principal safety
hazards performed when the product is first conceived.
Choice 4 is correct.

76. Inherent or intrinsic reliability

1. is that reliability which can be improved only
   by design change.

2. can be improved only by an improvement in the
   state of the art.

3. is that reliability estimated over a stated period
   of time by a stated measurement technique.

4. is not an estimated reliability.

Inherent reliability is obtained by eliminating assignable
causes of failure. Once this level is achieved failures occur
at random and reliability can only be improved by design
change, choice 1.

77. Reliability prediction is

1. the process of estimating performance.

2. the process of estimating the probability that
   a product will perform its intended function
   for a stated time.

3. the process of telling "how you can get there

from here."

4. All of the above.

Reliability is defined as the probability that a product will perform its intended function for a stated period of time. Reliability prediction is an attempt to estimate reliability, choice 2.

78. Maintainability is

1. the probability of a system being restored to functional operation within a given period of time.

2. performing adequate maintenance on a system.

3. probability of survival of a system for a given period of time.

4. maintaining a machine in satisfactory working condition.

5. None of the above.

Choice 1 is the definition of maintainability.

79. Quality assurance plans for computer software packages should include all of the following elements except

1. accurate and complete documentation of programs.

2. test criteria and test procedures.

3. provision of alternate packages.

4. testing under real life conditions.

Choice 3 is not an appropriate quality assurance element.

     80. Basic sources of reliability data are

        A. In-plant testing.

        B. Field testing.

        C. Operation by user.

        1. A and B

        2. B and C

        3. A and C

        4. A, B and C

All of the selections are common sources of reliability data, choice 4.

     81. Complaint indices should

        1. recognize the degree of dissatisfaction as viewed

           by the customer.

        2. provide a direct input to corrective action.

        3. not necessarily be based on field complaints or

           dollar values of claims paid or on service calls.

        4. ignore life cycle costs.

A valid complaint index must somehow measure the degree of customer dissatisfaction. A mildly dissatisfied customer may still buy your product; an extremely dissatisfied customer may discourage others from buying your product. Thus choice 1 is best.

The only possible alternate choice is choice 2. It can be argued that while complaint indices can be used in corrective action, they don't in and of themselves provide direct input into this process. In fact, the input is often quite indirect.

    82. Effective Automated Data Processing is

        1. a process which uses punch cards to sort, compile and analyze data.

        2. a process in which computers are used to analyze data.

        3. a process, largely self-regulating, in which information is handled with a minimum of human effort and intervention.

        4. a process in which records are classified, sorted, computed, summarized, transmitted and stored.

        5. None of the above.

Choice 3 is clearly best. Choices 1, 2, and 4 describe attributes of automated data processing systems, but these systems could well be quite ineffective.

    83. When using a hand held programmable calculator to compute the adjusted sum of squares for a variable, the formula $[\Sigma(x^2) - (\overline{X})\Sigma x]$ is preferred to $[\Sigma(x^2) - (\Sigma x)^2/N]$ because

1. $\overline{X}$ has already been calculated.

2. the preferred formula is significantly easier
   to compute.

3. there is less chance of underflow or overflow.

4. division by N may produce a rounding error.

Choice 3 is the best one given. Most modern programmable calculators carry 10 to 13 digits in their calculations, which can be inadequate when working with the squares of sums of measurements having 6 or more significant digits.

84. Analysis of data on all product returns is
    important because

    1. failure rates change with length of product
       usage.

    2. changes in design and in customer use are often
       well reflected.

    3. immediate feedback and analysis of product
       performance becomes available.

    4. All of the above.

    5. None of the above.

Analysis of data on all product returns is important for all the reasons given, thus choice 4 should be selected. Note that choice 5 <u>can't</u> be right because "all of the above" is one of the above!

85. A successful quality circle program should produce

all of the following benefits **except**

1. improved worker morale.

2. decreased need for management efforts to main-

tain quality.

3. improved communication between managers and

quality circle members.

4. cost **savings** from participative problem solving.

No quality program decreases the need for management efforts
to maintain quality.   Choice 2 is correct.

86. The famous Hawthorne study provided the following

clinical evidence regarding the factors that can

increase work group productivity.

1. Attention and recognition are more important

than working conditions.

2. Productivity did not change significantly under

any of the test conditions.

3. Informal group pressures set a production "goal."

4. People with higher capabilities are bored with

routine jobs.

5. Work station layout is critical to higher

productivity.

The Hawthorne experiment involved a study where the working
environment was changed for a selected group and the effect

of the change was evaluated. The study found that the group's productivity improved <u>regardless</u> <u>of</u> <u>how</u> <u>the</u> <u>environment</u> <u>was</u> <u>changed</u>! The conclusion was that the improvement was the result of the special attention and recognition the selected groups received, choice 1.

> 87. Which of the following is NOT a management
>
>   initiated error?
>
>   1. The imposition of conflicting priorities.
>
>   2. The lack of operator capacity.
>
>   3. Management indifference or apathy.
>
>   4. Conflicting quality specifications.
>
>   5. Work space, equipment and environment.

If we assume that "lack of operator capacity" means the operator is inherently incapable of performing acceptably in spite of adequate training and resources, then choice 2 is correct.

> 88. Which one of these human management approaches
>
>   has led to the practice of job enrichment?
>
>   1. Skinner.
>
>   2. Maslow.
>
>   3. Herzberg's "Hygiene Theory."
>
>   4. McGregor.

Herzberg's Hygiene Theory postulates that "satisfiers" and "dissatisfiers" are not opposites, rather they are separate scales altogether. "Satisfiers" are motivators that can result in improved performance. Dissatisfiers are "hygiene factors" that must be dealt with if motivation is to be effective. Some examples are shown below.

HYGIENE THEORY

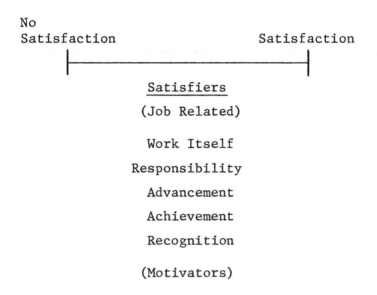

Satisfiers

(Job Related)

Work Itself

Responsibility

Advancement

Achievement

Recognition

(Motivators)

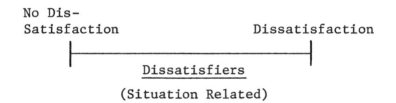

Dissatisfiers

(Situation Related)

Company Policy and Administration

Supervision

Salary

Interpersonal Relations

Working Conditions

(Hygiene Factors)

While choice 3 is correct here, it is important that you review the theories of Skinner, Maslow, and McGregor as well. B.F. Skinner is a behaviorist who studied operant conditioning. Maslow is famous for his need hierarchy (below).

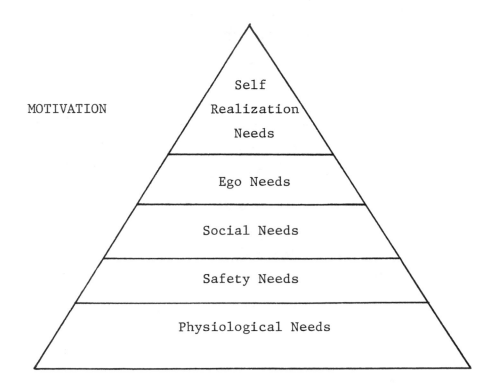

MOTIVATION

Self Realization Needs

Ego Needs

Social Needs

Safety Needs

Physiological Needs

Need Hierarchy

A. S. Maslow

Brandeis University

McGregor is known for theories X and Y:

> Theory X - Employees are basically greedy, lazy, and uncooperative. Motivation should be in the form of pay penalties and incentives, disciplinary action, etc.

Theory Y - Employees are self-motivated; but
they may lack the proper training
and tools to do their job.

89. Extensive research into the results of quality
motivation has shown that
1. the supervisor's attitude towards his people
is of little long term consequence.
2. motivation is too nebulous to be correlated
with results.
3. motivation is increased when employees set
their own goals.
4. motivation is increased when management sets
challenging goals slightly beyond the attainment of the better employees.

Choices 1, 2, and 4 have been shown to be _false_. Choice 3 is
correct.

90. Select the non-hygienic motivator, as defined by Maslow.
1. Salary increases.
2. Longer vacations.
3. Improved medical plan.
4. Sales bonuses.
5. Performance recognition.

Choice 5 is obviously correct.

APPLICATIONS

1. A study was conducted on the relationship between
   the speed of different cars and their gasoline
   mileage. The correlation coefficient was found
   to be 0.35. Later, it was discovered that there
   was a defect in the speedometers and they had all
   been set 5 miles per hour too fast. The correlation coefficient was computed using the corrected
   scores. Its new value will be

   1. 0.30

   2. 0.35

   3. 0.40

   4. -.35

The simple correlation coefficient is given by the equation

$$r = \frac{\sum\limits_{i=1}^{n} (Xi - \overline{X})(Yi - \overline{Y})}{\sqrt{\sum\limits_{i=1}^{n} (Xi - \overline{X})^2 \sum\limits_{i=1}^{n} (Yi - \overline{Y})^2}}$$

An illustration is shown below

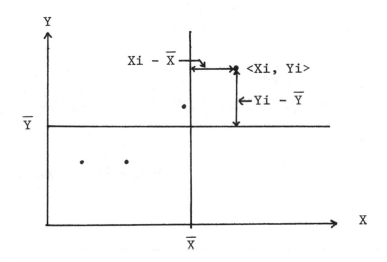

If all the speedometers are set 5 m.p.h. too fast it would
have the effect of shifting all Yi's down by 5 units. How-
ever, $\overline{Y}$ would also drop by 5 so the <u>sums</u> <u>of</u> <u>differences</u>
(Yi - $\overline{Y}$) would not change. Also, the sums of differences
Xi - $\overline{X}$ are unchanged by the defect. Therefore r is unchanged
and remains .35, choice 2.

2. A two-way Analysis of Variance has r levels for

the one variable and c levels for the second variable

with 2 observations per cell. The degrees of freedom

for interaction is

1. 2 (r × c)

2. (r - 1) (c - 1)

3. rc - 1

4. 2 (r - 1) (c - 1)

The degrees of freedom for interaction for two-way Analysis
of Variance is always (r - 1) (c - 1), regardless of the

number of observations per cell. Choice 2 is correct.

3. For a certain maker of car, the factory-installed
   brake linings have a mean lifetime of 40,000 miles
   with a 5,000 mile standard deviation. A sample of
   100 cars has been selected for testing. Assuming
   that the finite population correction may be
   ignored, the standard error of $\overline{X}$ is

   1. 50 miles.

   2. 500 miles.

   3. 400 miles.

   4. 4,000 miles.

The standard error of the mean is given by

$$S_{\overline{X}} = S/\sqrt{n} \quad \text{where } S = \text{Standard deviation of individuals}$$
$$n = \text{The sample size}$$

For this problem S = 5000 and n = 100, thus

$$S_{\overline{X}} = \frac{5000}{\sqrt{100}} = 500$$

Choice 2.

4. You have been asked to sample a lot of 300 units
   from a vendor whose past quality has been about
   2% defective. A sample of 40 pieces is drawn from
   the lot and you have been told to reject the lot if
   you find two or more parts defective. What is the
   probability of finding two or more parts defective?

1. .953

2. .809

3. .191

4. .047

The exact probability can be found using the binomial distribution, assuming continuous production. However, the Poisson distribution should give an adequate--and much faster--approximation. We first compute

$$np = 40 \times .02 = 0.8$$

And then recall that

$$Prob\ (2\ or\ more) = 1 - Prob\ (1\ or\ less)$$

This is important because the probability of X _or_ _less_ is given by most poisson tables. Entering the table we find

$$Prob\ (1\ or\ less) = .809$$

Thus

$$Prob\ (2\ or\ more) = 1 - .809 = .191$$

Choice 3.

5. What is the probability of finding no defective items in a random sample of 100 items taken from the output of a continuous process which averages 0.7% defective items?

1. 0.49

2. 1.74

3. 0.10

    4. 0.74

    5. 0.33

Again, the poisson should be tried first due to the speed with which one can obtain a result; however, the exact distribution is the binomial. We compute

$$np = 100 \times .7\% = 100 \times .007 = .7$$

And entering the poisson tables we find

$$\text{Prob } (0) = .497$$

Choice 1 is the only one close.

    6. What is the standard deviation of the following

       sample; 3.2, 3.1, 3.3, 3.3, 3.1?

       1. 3.2

       2. 0.0894

       3. 0.1

       4. 0.0498

       5. 0.2

The sample standard deviation is given by

$$s = \sqrt{\frac{\sum\limits_{i=1}^{n} (X_i^2) - \overline{X} \left(\sum\limits_{i=1}^{n} X_i\right)}{n-1}}$$

For these data

i	Xi	Xi^2
1	3.2	10.24
2	3.1	9.61
3	3.3	10.89
4	3.3	10.89
5	3.1	9.61
sum	16	51.24

$$\overline{X} = \frac{16}{5} = 3.2 \ , \ n = 5$$

$$s = \sqrt{\frac{51.24 - 3.2(16)}{5-1}} = .1$$

Choice #3.

Anyone taking the CQE exam should have a pocket calculator that computes $\overline{X}$ and s automatically.

Lots of 75 parts each are inspected to an AQL of 0.2%
using normal inspection, single sampling. A single
lower specification limit, denoted by 'L,' is used.
The standard level (Level II in MIL-STD-105D, Level IV
in MIL-STD-414) is specified.
Note: Please refer to the above dialog for the
following three (3) questions.

The next three (3) questions require that you have a copy of
MIL-STD-105D and MIL-STD-414 handy.

7. The sample size for MIL-STD-105D is

    1. 13

    2. 32

    3. 50

    4. 75

To get the answer to question 7 we begin by entering Table I for a lot size of 75, Level II inspection. We find sample size code letter E.

Table I - Sample Size Code Letters

Lot or Batch Size	Special Inspection Levels				General Inspection Levels		
	S-1	S-2	S-3	S-4	I	II	III
26 to 50	A	B	B	C	C	D	E
51 t0 90	B	B	C	C	C	E	F
91 to 150	B	B	C	D	D	F	G

This value is taken to Table II-A where we find the row for Code Letter E and the column for .25% AQL.

Table II-A - Single Sampling Plans for Normal Inspection

(Master Table)

Sample Size Code Letter	Sample Size	AQL's					
		0.15		0.25		0.40	
		Ac	Re	Ac	Re	Ac	Re

D	8			
E	13			
F	20			
G	32			
H	50		0 1	0 1
J	80	0 1		

The arrows take us from the code letter E row to the code letter H row, for the sample size of 50. Choice 3.

8. The sample size for MIL-STD-414, estimating

variability by the range method, is

1. 3

2. 7

3. 10

4. 15

5. 20

MIL-STD-414 is the department of defense standard for inspection by variables for percent defective. A good analysis of the standard can be found in

> Kao, John H.K., "MIL-STD-414 Sampling Procedures and Tables for Inspection by Variables for Percent Defective," Journal of Quality Technology, Vol. 3, No. 1, January 1971.

Several past CQE exams have had questions that require an understanding of this standard.

We begin to answer question 8 by entering Table A-2

TABLE A-2

Sample Size Code Letters

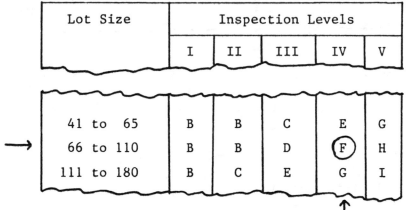

Lot Size	Inspection Levels				
	I	II	III	IV	V
41 to 65	B	B	C	E	G
66 to 110	B	B	D	(F)	H
111 to 180	B	C	E	G	I

Our next step is to enter Table C-1 (we assume variability unknown since we are not told otherwise).

TABLE C-1

Master Table for Normal and Tightened Inspection:
Variability Unknown

(Single Specification Limit--Form 1)

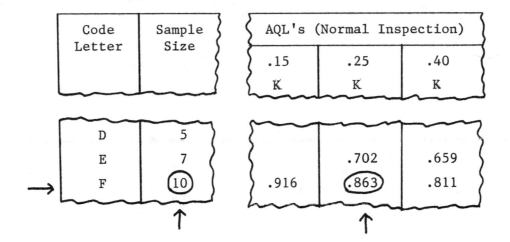

We get our sample size as 10, which is choice 3.

9. The acceptance criterion, using MIL-STD-414 and

the range method is:

Accept the lot if

1. $(\overline{X} - L)/R \geq 0.702$

2. $(\overline{X} - L)/R \geq 0.863$

3. $(\overline{X} - L)/R \geq 1.06$

4. $(\overline{X} - L)/R \leq 1.06$

Refer to the Table shown in question 8. When form 1, section C, is used the acceptance criterion is

$(\overline{X} - L)/R \geq K$

The Table above gives K = .863, choice 2.

10. A process is producing material which is 30%
defective. Five pieces are selected at random
for inspection. What is the probability of
exactly two good pieces being found in the sample?

1. .868

2. .309

3. .436

4. .132

We will use the binomial distribution to get

$$\text{Prob }(x) = \binom{n}{x}\ p^x\ (1-p)^{n-x}$$

where x = The number of good pieces

n = The sample size

p = The proportion good

$$\text{Prob }(x = 2) = \binom{5}{2}\ (.7)^2\ (1-.7)^{5-2}$$

$$= \frac{5!}{2!3!}\ (.49)\ (.027) = .1323$$

Choice 4 is closest.

11. An inspection plan is set up to randomly sample
3 ft.^{2} of a 1,000 ft.^{2} carpet and to accept the
carpet only if no flaws are found in the 3 ft.^{2}
sample. What is the probability that a roll of
carpet with an average of one (1) flaw per square
foot will be rejected by the plan?

> 1. .05
>
> 2. .72
>
> 3. .90
>
> 4. .95

The correct distribution is the poisson. The parameter we need to use the table is λ, found as follows:

> Defects per unit = 1
>
> Units per sample = 3
>
> λ = Defects per unit $\times$ Units per sample = 3

The roll will be rejected if we find 1 or more defects in our sample. Thus

> Prob (rej) = 1 - Prob (0 defects)

Entering the poisson table with λ = 3 we find

> Prob (0) = .05

Thus

> Prob (rej) = 1 - .05 = .95

Choice 4.

> 12. A process is in control at $\bar{\bar{X}}$ = 100, $\bar{R}$ = 7.3 with
>
> n = 4. If the process level shifts to 101.5, with
>
> the same $\bar{R}$, what is the probability that the next
>
> $\bar{X}$ point will fall outside the old control limits?
>
> 1. .016
>
> 2. .029
>
> 3. .122
>
> 4. .360

Since sample means are normally distributed we will use normal tables to get the probability. We must compute Z to enter these tables, where

$$Z = \frac{\text{Limit} - \bar{\bar{X}}}{\sigma/\sqrt{n}}$$

For a controlled process we can use the estimate of σ

$$\hat{\sigma} = \bar{R}/d_2$$

We find d_2 in a table of factors for control charts at n = 4 is d_2 = 2.059. Thus

$$\hat{\sigma} = 7.3/2.059 = 3.56$$

If the shift in $\bar{\bar{X}}$ is upward then the probability of an $\bar{X}$ being below the lower limit is negligible. Thus we will only consider the probability of exceeding an upper limit. Before the shift our upper control limit (UCL) was

$$UCL = \bar{\bar{X}} + A_2\bar{R}$$

where A_2 is obtained from control chart

factor tables at n = 4 as .729. Thus

$$UCL = 100 + .729\ (7.3) = 105.3217 \cong 105.3$$

This gives

$$Z = \frac{105.3 - 101.5}{3.56/\sqrt{4}} = 2.13$$

Using normal tables we find

$$\text{Prob}\ (\bar{X} > 105.3) = \text{Prob}\ (Z > 2.13) = .016$$

Choice 1.

13. The following coded results were obtained from

a single factor, completely randomized experiment,

in which the production outputs of the three machines

(A, B, C) were to be compared.

A.   4   8   5   7   6

B.   2   0   1   2   4

C. -3   1 -2 -1   0

What is the sum of squares for the error term?

1. 170

2. 130

3. 40

4. 14

This will illustrate the calculations for the one-way
Analysis of Variance (ANOVA) for the completely randomized
single factor experiment:

		Total	n	Sum of Squares
Treatment A	4, 8, 5, 7, 6	30	5	190
Treatment B	2, 0, 1, 2, 4	9	5	25
Treatment C	-3, 1, -2, -1, 0	-5	5	15
	Totals	34	15	230

Total Sum of Squares = $230 - \frac{(34)^2}{15} = 152.933$

Treatment Sum of Squares

$= \frac{(30)^2}{5} + \frac{(9)^2}{5} + \frac{(-5)^2}{5} - \frac{(34)^2}{15} = 124.133$

Error Sum of Squares

= Total Sum of Squares − Treatment Sum of Squares

= 152.933 − 124.133 = 28.8

The ANOVA Table is given below

Source	Sum of Squares	D.F.	Mean Squares	F
Machines	124.133	2	62.067	25.86
Error	28.800	12	2.400	--
Total	152.933	14	--	--

The probability that F is due to chance is less than .01.

The answer given in the published exam is incorrect.

More information on ANOVA can be found in

> Hicks, C.R., Fundamental Concepts in the Design of Experiments, 2nd Ed., Holt, Reinhart and Winston, 1973, New York.

14. What value of z in the normal tables has 5% of the

   area in the tail beyond it?

   1. 1.960

   2. 1.645

   3. 2.576

   4. 1.282

The correct answer is 2. Some common z values and their associated percentages are given below:

Z	% Beyond
2.576	.5
2.325	1.0
1.960	2.5
1.645	5.0
1.282	10.0

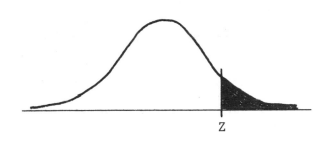

15. An $\overline{X}$ and R chart was prepared for an operation using twenty samples with five pieces in each sample. $\overline{\overline{X}}$ was found to be 33.6 and $\overline{R}$ was 6.20. During production a sample of five was taken and the pieces measured 36, 43, 37, 25, and 38. At the time this sample was taken

1. both average and range were within control limits.

2. neither average nor range were within control limits.

3. only the average was outside control limits.

4. only the range was outside control limits.

We find the control limits are

Range Chart

$$LCL_R = D_3\overline{R} = 0 \times 6.2 = 0$$
$$UCL_R = D_4\overline{R} = 2.114 \times 6.2 = 13.1$$

Averages Chart

$$LCL_{\overline{X}} = \overline{\overline{X}} - A_2\overline{R} = 33.6 - .577 \times 6.2 = 30.0$$
$$UCL_{\overline{X}} = \overline{\overline{X}} + A_2\overline{R} = 33.6 + .577 \times 6.2 = 37.2$$

For the 5 piece sample

$$\overline{X} = 35.8$$

$$R = 18$$

Thus $\overline{X}$ is in control, R is not; choice 4.

16. A comparison of known sigma and unknown sigma
    variables plans will show that equal protection
    is obtained (as determined by the OC curves)

    1. when the unknown sigma sample size is smaller
       than the known sigma sample size.

    2. when the known sigma sample size is larger
       than the unknown sigma size.

    3. when the known sigma and unknown sigma sample
       sizes are equal.

    4. None of these.

In general, less data is required for equal protection if
sigma is known. This selection is not offered, thus choice
4 is correct.

An electronics firm was experiencing high rejections
in their multiple connector manufacturing departments.
"P" charts were introduced as part of a program to
reduce defectives. Control limits were based on
prior history, using the formula:

$$P' \pm 3\sqrt{\frac{P'\ (100 - P')}{N}}$$

P' is the historical value of percent defective

and N is the number of pieces inspected each week.

After six weeks, the following record was accumulated.

Dept.	P'	Week 1	Week 2	Week 3	Week 4	Week 5	Week 6
104	9	8	11	6	13	12	10
105	16	13	19	20	12	15	17
106	15	18	19	16	11	13	16

17. 1000 pieces were inspected each week in each

department. Which department(s) exhibited a point

or points out of control during this period?

(Round off calculations to nearest tenth of a

percentage point.)

1. Department 104

2. Department 105

3. Department 106

4. All of the departments

5. None of the departments

The control limits for the three departments are

Dept. 104

$$LCL_p = 9 - 3\sqrt{\frac{9(100 - 9)}{1000}} = 6.3\%$$

$$UCL_p = 9 + 3\sqrt{\frac{9(100 - 9)}{1000}} = 11.7\%$$

Dept. 105

$$LCL_p = 16 - 3\sqrt{\frac{16(100 - 16)}{1000}} = 12.5\%$$

$$UCL_p = 16 + 3\sqrt{\frac{16(100 - 16)}{1000}} = 19.5\%$$

Dept. 106

$$LCL_p = 15 - 3 \sqrt{\frac{15(100 - 15)}{1000}} = 11.6\%$$

$$UCL_p = 15 + 3 \sqrt{\frac{15(100 - 15)}{1000}} = 18.4\%$$

When these are compared to the data given we find

Dept. 104: Below LCL_p at week 3

Above UCL_p at weeks 4 and 5

Dept. 105: Below LCL_p at week 4

Above UCL_p at week 3

Dept. 106: Below LCL_p at week 4

Above UCL_p at week 2

Thus choice 4 is correct.

---

18. A large lot of parts is rejected by your customer and found, upon screening, to be 20% defective. What is the probability that the lot would have been accepted by the following sampling plan: sample size = 10; accept if no defectives; reject if one or more defectives?

1. .89

2. .20

3. .80

4. .11

5. None of the above

The easiest way to compute this is to note that for sampling with replacement ("large lot")

$$\text{Prob (0 defective)} = \text{Prob (\#1 good) Prob (\#2 good)}$$
$$. . . \text{Prob (\#10 good)}$$
$$= (1 - .2)^{10} = .107 \cong .11$$

Choice 4.

19. Consider the SS and MS columns of an Analysis

of Variance table for a single factor design.

The appropriate ratio for testing the null

hypothesis of no treatment effect is

1. SS treatments divided by SS residual.

2. MS treatments divided by MS residual.

3. SS treatments divided by MS residual.

4. MS treatments divided by SS residual.

Refer again to the example shown for question 13, the correct choice is #2. Note that the terms "residual" and "error" are synonomous.

20. Which table should be used to determine a

confidence interval on the mean when σ is not

known and the sample size is 10?

1. z

2. t

3. F

4. x^2

The t tables are used to place confidence bounds on the mean based on small sample sizes. The bounds are

$$\overline{X} - t_{1-\alpha/2} \frac{s}{\sqrt{n}} < \mu < \overline{X} + t_{1-\alpha/2} \frac{s}{\sqrt{n}}$$

Choice 2 is correct.

21. The results of a designed experiment are to be analyzed using a Chi-square test. There are five treatments under consideration and each observation falls into one of two categories (success or failure). The calculated value of Chi-square is compared to the tabulated Chi-square with how many degrees of freedom?

    1. 10
    2. 9
    3. 5
    4. 4

The degrees of freedom for analysis of contingency tables with r rows and c columns is (r-1)(c-1). In this problem we have 2 rows and 5 columns (or vice-versa)

	TREATMENT				
	1	2	3	4	5
Good					
Bad					

Thus   df = (2-1)(5-1) = 4

Choice 4.

A thorough discussion of this type of analysis is given in Chapter 28 of

> Duncan, A.J., <u>Quality Control and Industrial Statistics</u>, Fourth Edition, Homewood, Illinois, Richard D. Irwen Inc., 1974.

22. Using MIL-STD-105D, what sample size should be taken from a lot of 1000 pieces for inspection level II with normal inspection?

   1. 32

   2. 50

   3. 80

   4. 100

   5. 125

Actually this question is missing some important items; these are

   · Single, double, or multiple sampling?

   · What AQL?

(For a proper question on MIL-STD-105D see #7 of this section.)

If we just find the sample size code letter (see question #7) and use this in the master table for single normal sampling, we get a sample size of 80. This is the "official" answer, choice 3.

Mini-Case Study

A certain equipment manufacturer offers warranty on his product for a period of one year after installation. His investigation revealed the following additional information:

	Mean	STD Dev
Time lag from date of production to date of sale (to dealer or distributor)	10 weeks	3 weeks
Time lag from date of sale to date of installation	14 weeks	3.5 weeks
Time lag from date of installation to date of processing warranty claim	30 weeks	10 weeks

Each of these time lags is normally distributed, and each is independent of the other. (For example, time to failure is independent of equipment age at time of installation.)

In February of last year, this manufacturer produced 4,000 units of a particular model. Through December of the same year (45 weeks), a total of 23 warranty claims had been processed on these 4,000 units.

Please refer to the above dialogue for the following three (3) questions. Carry all calculations to **three** places.

23. The standard deviation of total time from date of production to date of processing claims is

    1. ten (10) weeks.

    2. eleven (11) weeks.

    3. thirteen and one-half (13.5) weeks.

    4. sixteen and one-half (16.5) weeks.

The needed statistical relation is

$$\sigma^2_{sum} = \text{Sum of individual } \sigma^2.$$

For this problem

$$\sigma_{total\ lag} = \sqrt{3^2 + 3.5^2 + 10^2} = 11.01 \text{ weeks}$$

Choice 2.

24. What proportion of the likely total (eventual) number of warranty claims on February's production has been processed through December?

    1. 0.186

    2. 0.207

    3. 0.468

    4. 0.532

    5. 0.793

To answer this we need to know the additional things

      · The mean of the sum = the sum of the means.

      · The sum of independent normally distributed
        random variables is normally distributed.

The mean time between production and processing is

$$\overline{X}_{total\ lag} = 10 + 14 + 30 = 54\ weeks$$

There are 45 weeks from the end of February through the end of December. We already know $\sigma_{total\ lag}$ from question 23. What we are asked, therefore, is

      "What proportion of a normally distributed
      variable with a mean = 54 and σ = 11 will be
      below X = 44?"

We compute

$$Z = \frac{X - \overline{X}}{\sigma} = \frac{45 - 54}{11} = -.82$$

and enter the normal tables to get

      Proportion = .206

Which is closest to choice 2.

<u>Proportion of Claims Processed</u>

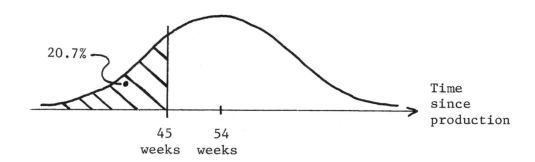

25. How many of these units are likely to eventually
    result in warranty claims?

    1. 28

    2. 55

    3. 88

    4. 111

    5. 152

Since 23 claims have been processed, and this is 20.7% of the
expected total

$$\text{Expected Total} = \frac{23}{.207} = 111 \text{ claims.}$$

Choice 4.

---

26. A process is checked by inspection of random samples
    of four shafts after a polishing operation, and $\overline{X}$
    and R charts are maintained. A person making a spot
    check picks out two shafts, measures them accurately,
    and plots the value of each on the $\overline{X}$ chart. Both
    points fall just outside the control limits. He
    advises the department foreman to stop the process.
    This decision indicates that

    1. the process level is out of control.

    2. both the level and dispersion are out of control.

    3. the process level is out of control but not the
       dispersion.

    4. the person is not using the chart correctly.

The person plotted <u>individual</u> readings on a chart for <u>averages</u>. He is not using the chart correctly, choice 4.

27. In performing an Analysis of Variance for a single

factor experiment, a fundamental assumption which

is made is that the factor

1. means are equal.

2. means are unequal.

3. variances are equal.

4. variances are unequal.

Homogeniety of variance, choice 3, is a fundamental assumption underlying Analysis of Variance. Also see question 15 in the Principles Section.

28. A purchaser wants to determine whether or not

there is any difference between the means of the

convolute paperboard cans supplied by two differ-

ent vendors, A and B. A random sample of 100

cans is selected from the output of each vendor.

The sample from A yielded a mean of 13.59 with a

standard deviation of 5.94. The sample from B

yielded a mean of 14.43 with a standard deviation

of 5.61. Which of the following would be a

suitable null hypothesis to test?

1. $\mu_A = \mu_B$

2. $\mu_A > \mu_B$

3. $\mu_A < \mu_B$

4. $\mu_A \neq \mu_B$

The question states: "A purchaser wants to determine whether or not there is any difference between the means . . ." The null hypothesis $\mu_A = \mu_B$ is correct. Choice 1.

29. The most important step in vendor certification

   is to

   1. obtain copies of vendor's handbook.

   2. familiarize vendor with quality requirements.

   3. analyze vendor's first shipment.

   4. visit the vendor's plant.

If the vendor isn't familiar with your requirements, chances are he won't meet them, even if he can. Choice 2 is correct.

30. Which of the following purposes are served by

   replicating an experiment?

      A. Provide a means for estimating the

         experimental error.

      B. Increase the number of treatments included

         in the experiment.

      C. Improve the precision of estimates of treat-

         ment effects.

   1. A and B only

   2. A and C only

3. B and C only

4. A, B and C

Increasing the number of observations by replicating an experiment provides the benefits described by A and C; this means choice 2 is correct. Another way to arrive at this is to observe that B is untrue and that only choice 2 doesn't have B.

31. Three trainees were given the same lot of 50 pieces and asked to classify them as defective or non-defective, with the following results:

	Trainee #1	Trainee #2	Trainee #3	Total
Defective	17	30	25	72
Non-Defective	33	20	25	78
Total	50	50	50	150

In determining whether or not there is a difference in the ability of the three trainees to properly classify the parts,

1. the value of Chi-square is about 6.

2. using a level of significance of 0.05, the critical value of Chi-square is 5.99.

3. since the obtained Chi-square is greater than 5.99, we reject the null hypothesis.

4. All of the above.

5. None of the above.

Refer to question 21 of this section for a reference that describes the method used to analyze the data. We first note that

$$\text{degrees of freedom} = (r-1)(c-1) = 2$$

and that Chi-square tables give a critical value of 5.97 for $\alpha = .05$. The Chi-square statistic is

$$\chi^2 = \frac{\Sigma \, (\text{Fo} - \text{Fe})^2}{\text{Fe}}$$

where Fo = The frequency observed in each cell

Fe = The frequency expected in each cell.

The sum is taken over all cells. Each cell Fe is computed as

$$\text{Fe (cell)} = \frac{\text{Row Total} \times \text{Column Total}}{\text{Grand Total}}$$

This gives the table below

EXPECTED FREQUENCIES

	Trainee #1	Trainee #2	Trainee #3
Defective	$\frac{50 \times 72}{150} = 24$	24	24
Non-Defective	$\frac{50 \times 78}{150} = 26$	26	26

$$\chi^2 = \frac{(17-24)^2}{24} + \frac{(30-24)^2}{24} + \frac{(25-24)^2}{24} + \frac{(33-26)^2}{26} + \frac{(20-26)^2}{26}$$

$$+ \frac{(25-26)^2}{26} = 6.89$$

Obviously choices 2 and 3 are correct. If we accept that 6.89 is "about 6" the answer is given by choice 4, which is the official answer.

32. The following measurements for a sample with Dimension X are representative of a process known to be in statistical control.

　　　42, 52, 64, 45, 53, 56, 70, 57, 49, 62

Which of the following best approximates the upper and lower control limits of the process capability? (Use generally accepted sigma-limits for the United States.)

1. 81 & 29

2. 59 & 51

3. 64 & 46

4. 70 & 42

When n = 10 the process capability of 6σ can be approximated as 2R. This set of data yields the following

$\overline{X}$ = 55

R = 70 - 42 = 28

Thus the limits are

Lower Limit = 55 - 28 = 27

Upper Limit = 55 + 28 = 83

This gives choice 1 as the closest, which is correct.

If the reader has a pocket calculator, he can compute (see
question #6 in this section)

$$s = 8.679$$

And use this to get

Lower Limit = $\overline{X}$ - 3s = 55 - 26 = 29

Upper Limit = $\overline{X}$ + 3s = 55 + 26 = 81

Which is the same as choice 1.

33. The prime use of a control chart is to

1. detect assignable causes of variation in the

    process.

2. detect nonconforming product.

3. measure the performance of all quality char-

    acteristics of a process.

4. detect the presence of random variation in

    the process.

Choice 1 describes Walter Shewhart's main reason for invent-
ing the control chart technique.

34. "Determine the flux meter reading of the part per

    specification." This inspection instruction violates

    which of the following guiding principles?

    A. The inspection method should be stated in

        operational terms.

    B. A specific objective should be established

        for each instruction.

1. A only

2. B only

3. A and B

4. Neither A nor B

A cardinal rule of inspection is that the method must be given in operational terms. According to W. Edwards Deming,*

"An operational definition consists of

(1) a criterion to be applied to an object or

to a group,

(2) a test of the object or of the group,

(3) decision: yes or no: the object or the

group did or did not meet the criterion."

The instruction given does not meet these three criteria. Choice 1 is correct.

35. If a test data does not support a Quality Engineer's

expectations, the best thing to do is

1. adjust the data to support expectations if it is

only slightly off.

2. draw the expected conclusion omitting that data not

supporting it.

3. re-evaluate the expectations of the test based

upon the data.

---

*Deming, W. Edwards, Quality Productivity and Competitive Position, MIT, Cambridge, MA, 1982.

4. report the data and expected conclusion with no

reference to one another.

It is common to find that the data do not support advance
expectations. When this happens one should carefully check
the accuracy and validity of the data. If the data are
correct, the only rational action is to reevaluate the expectations, choice 3.

36. In deciding whether sampling inspection of parts

would be more economical than 100% inspection,

you need to determine all of the following **except**

1. cost of inspecting the parts.

2. cost of correcting defective parts.

3. cost of <u>not</u> finding defective parts.

4. cost of improving the production process.

Inspection, by acceptance sampling methods or by 100% screening, is a <u>detection</u> oriented activity that is taken based on
the currect process. The correct choice is number 4. This
is not to say that the process shouldn't be improved, process
improvement should be an ongoing activity. In fact, it can
be shown that under quite general conditions the optimal
amount of inspection is <u>always</u> either 100% inspection or zero
inspection. This is discussed by Deming (see question #34
for the reference); a proof is given in

Lindsay, G.F. and Bishop, A.B., "Allocation of Screening Inspection Effort--A Dynamic Programming Approach," <u>Management Science</u>, Vol. 10, No. 2, January 1964, pp. 342-352.

37. Pre-control starts a process specifically centered between

   1. process limits.

   2. safety lines.

   3. normal distribution limits.

   4. three-sigma control limits.

   5. specification limits.

Pre-control is a specification based process control scheme. Pre-control begins by assuming that a process is just capable of meeting specifications and is normally distributed. This condition is illustrated below

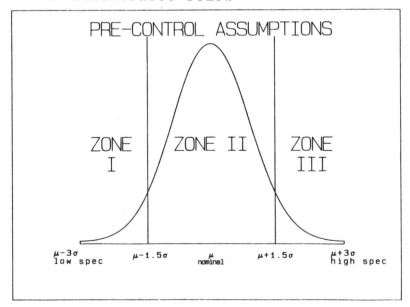

The process is exactly centered between the specification limits and the inherent variation of the process, 6 standard

deviations, is exactly equal to the tolerance. The Pre-Control rules are

1. Begin with 100% inspection.

2. If a piece is out of specification, reset the process.

3. If the piece is in Zone I or Zone III, do not adjust the process but check the next piece.

   a. If the second piece is in the same zone, reset the process and return to step 1.

   b. If the second piece is beyond the opposite Pre-Control line (e.g. Zone I followed by Zone III or vice-versa), take action to reduce variability and return to step 1.

4. When five (5) consecutive pieces fall in Zone II, begin checking on a sample basis. Usually the sample frequency begins at 1 in 5 and is adjusted so that a process is adjusted about once for every 25 inspections. Each sample result is processed through steps 2 and 3.

Choice 5 is correct.

38. A technique whereby various product features are graded as to relative importance is called

   1. classification of defects.

   2. quality engineering.

   3. classification of characteristics.

    4. feature grading.

The question describes classification of characteristics, choice 3. This is an essential activity whose purpose is to separate the vital few characteristics from the trivial many so that an effective allocation of resources is possible. Classification of defects is also quite common. The prospective CQE should be familiar with the defect classifications in MIL-STD-105D, paragraph 2.

39. The laboratory has notified the Quality Engineer of an incoming product which has changed from acceptable to marginal over a period of six months. Which of the following actions should taken?

A. Notify the laboratory to check their analysis and send a sample to an outside laboratory to verify the results.

B. Notify the supplier of your observations and concern about the acceptability of his product.

C. Notify receiving to reject the product based on the product's trend toward unacceptability.

1. A and B only

2. A and C only

3. B and C only

4. A, B and C

Again, as happens so often, option C is not correct (the product is <u>marginal</u>, not yet unacceptable) and choice 1 is the only one that doesn't include this option. Thus choice 1 is correct.

40. One of the major hazards in the Material Review Board procedure is the tendency of the board to emphasize only the disposition function and to neglect the

    _____ _____ function.

    1. statistical analysis

    2. corrective action

    3. material evaluation

    4. tolerance review

    5. manufacturing methods

The tendency of MRB's to underemphasize corrective action is both well known and unfortunate. Choice 2 is correct.

41. A certain part is produced in lot quantities of 1,000. Prior history shows that 90% of the production lots are 1% defective or better, but the remaining 10% range between 5% and 10% defective. A defective part costs $5 to repair at this point, but the same defect will average $80 if allowed to be installed in the next higher assembly. Inspection at the part level costs $1.50 per part, and rejected lots will be sorted at your expense. What inspection plan would you specify

for this part?

1. 100% inspection.

2. No inspection.

3. n = 32, A = 1, R = 2 (single-sampling).

4. n = 50, A = 0, R = 1 (single-sampling).

5. n = 5, A = 1, R = 2 (single-sampling).

The objective is to minimize the average total cost per lot, which is given by the equation

$$C = 1.5 \times ATI + 5 \times ATR + 80 \times ADI$$

where ATI = Average total inspected per lot.

ATR = Average total repaired per lot.

ADI = Average defectives installed at a higher assembly per lot. We'll assume 5% are 5% defective and 5% are 10% defective.

With 100% Inspection

ATI = 1000

ATR = .9(.01)(1000) + .05(.05)(1000) + .05(.10)(1000)

= 1000 [.9(.01) + .05(.05) + .05(.10)]

= 16.5

ADI = 0, assuming perfect inspection

and C = 1.5 (1000) + 5 (16.5) + 80 (0) = $\underline{\$1582.50}$

With No Inspection

ATI = 0

ATR = 0

ADI = 16.5 (same as ATR above)

and C = 1.5 (0) + 5 (0) + 80 (16.5) = \$1320.00

With n = 32, A = 1, R = 2

(Binomial distribution used to get probabilities)

ATI = .9 [32 + .04 (1000-32)] + .05 [32 + .48 (1000

-32)] + .05 [32 + .84 (1000-32)]

= 130.736

ATR = 16.5 - 10.74 = 5.76

ADI = [.9 (.96)(.01) + .05(.52)(.05)

+ .05(.16)(.10)] 1000 = 10.74

C = 1.5(130.736) + 5(5.76) + 80(10.74) = \$1084.10

Using similar methods for the other choices gives us the table below

Quality Control Scheme	ATI	ATR	ADI	Cost
100% Inspection	1000	16.5	0	\$1582.50
No inspection	0	0	16.5	1320.00
n=32, A=1, R=2	130.736	10.74	5.76	1084.10
n=50, A=0, R=1	478.825	10.84	5.66	1225.24
n= 5, A=1, R=2	11.08	0.47	16.03	1301.37

The least cost scheme is choice 3.

42. In product liability, the proper legal term for statements regarding the reliability of a product are known as

    1. advertisements.

    2. warranties.

    3. contracts.

    4. representations.

    5. obligations.

The definition of <u>representation</u> is

        "A statement of fact on the faith of which

        a contract is entered into."

Choice 4 is correct.

    43. In case of conflict between contract specifications

        and shop practice,

        1. company procedures normally prevail.

        2. arbitration is necessary.

        3. the customer is always right.

        4. good judgment should be exercised.

        5. contract specifications normally apply.

Choice 5 is correct.

    44. The provisions of the F.D.A. Regulations for thermally

        processed, low acid foods, packaged in hermetically

        sealed containers, require all of the following **except**

        1. copies of all production and laboratory records be

            kept for six (6) months then reviewed and destroyed

            by an authorized person.

2. incoming raw materials, ingredients and packaging components should be inspected upon receipt to ensure that they are suitable for processing.

3. scheduled processes for low acid foods shall be established by qualified persons having expert knowledge of thermal processing.

4. it is either destroyed or evaluated by a competent processing authority to detect any potential hazard to public health.

Assuming that most who are taking the CQE exam are not experts in every field, let me suggest that a way to approach this sort of question is to look for an obvious answer. In this case choice 1 is obviously correct because it is inconceivable that F.D.A. would require the destruction of all production and laboratory records after six (6) months.

45. Which of the following may be considered a justification for reinspection by the contractor of a lot which has been verified as nonconforming by the inspector?

1. Belief by the contractor that the random samples did not constitute a true picture of the lot.

2. The fact that the contractor had not produced to these specifications before.

3. Discovery that the scales used for inspection
   were out of adjustment.

4. None of the above.

Only choice 3 is justification. Choice 1 is a matter of (biased) opinion, choice 2 is irrelevant.

46. When conducting an inspection for surface cleanliness,
    a simple and effective means for detecting the presence
    of oils, grease, or waxes is

    1. stereomicroscopic inspection.

    2. the Aqueous Conductivity Test.

    3. the Liebermann-Storch Test.

    4. the Water-Break Test.

The water-break test is performed by placing water on the surface of the part or test piece and observing whether the water "sheets" or "beads up." Beading indicates contamination in the form of oils, grease, or waxes--much as water beading on your car hood indicates wax. Choice 4 is correct.

47. Creep is defined as that deformation occuring over
    a period of time with material subjected to

    1. fluctuating stress and fluctuating strap.

    2. constant temperature and a fluctuating stress.

    3. constant temperature with no stress.

    4. constant stress at a constant temperature.

The long-term effect of temperature is manifest in a phenomenon known as creep. If a tensile-type specimen is subjected to a fixed load at an elevated temperature, it will elongate continuously until rupture occurs, even though the applied stress is below the yield strength of the material at the temperature of testing. Although the rate of elongation is small, it is enough to be of great importance in the design of equipment that operates at high temperatures for long periods of time. Choice 4 is correct.

48. How should measurement standards be controlled?

   A. Develop a listing of measurement standards with nomenclature and number for control.

   B. Determine calibration intervals and calibration sources for measurement standards.

   C. Maintain proper environmental conditions and traceability of accuracy to National Bureau of Standards.

   1. A and B only

   2. A and C only

   3. B and C only

   4. A, B and C

All three options are necessary for measurement standards control; choice 4 is correct. The CQE should be familiar with MIL-STD-45662; MILITARY STANDARD calibration system requirements.

49. When making measurements with test instruments,

   precision and accuracy mean

   1. the same.

   2. the opposite.

   3. consistency and correctness, respectively.

   4. exactness and traceability, respectively.

   5. None of the above.

The terms "precision" and "accuracy" can be described using
an analogy to target shooting with a rifle. If your shots
are closely grouped, your shooting can be called precise,
regardless of how far your grouping is from the bullseye.
If the bullseye is at the center of the grouping your shooting is accurate, regardless of the scatter of the group. A
close grouping centered at the bullseye is both precise and
accurate. Obviously precise and consistent are synonomous,
as are accurate and correct; choice 3.

Precise but Not Accurate   Accurate but Not Precise

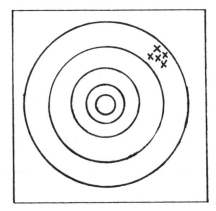
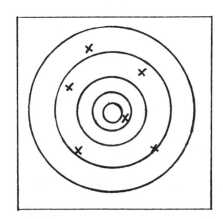

Accurate and Precise

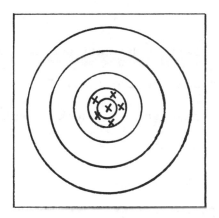

An excellent and thorough discussion of the concepts of pre-cision and accuracy can be found in

> Eisenhart, C., "Realistic Evaluation of the Precision and Accuracy of Instrument Cali-bration Systems," <u>Journal of Research of the NBS</u>, Vol. 67C, No. 2, April-June 1963.

50. The maximum stress to which a material may be sub-jected without any permanent deformation remaining upon complete release of stress is its

    1. ultimate yield.

    2. fatigue life.

    3. elastic limit.

    4. elastic hysteresis.

This is the definition of elastic limit, choice 3. By now you're beginning to see the value of a good technical dictionary.

51. A subsurface discontinuity in some purchased steel
    bar stock is a suspected cause for the high failure
    rate in your parts fabrication area. All of the
    following nondestructive test (NDT) methods could
    be used to screen the bar stock **except**

    1. magnetic particle testing.

    2. radiographic testing.

    3. liquid penetrant testing.

    4. eddy current testing.

    5. ultrasonic testing.

Liquid penetrant inspection works by <u>penetrating</u>. This implies that the discontinuity must be exposed, which is not the case with a subsurface discontinuity. Choice 3 is correct.

52. In attempting to replace human evaluation of foods
    in order to achieve objectivity, we must use, as an
    ultimate criterion of accuracy,

    1. gas chromatography.

    2. shear press.

    3. viscosimeter.

    4. None of the above.

One can successfully argue that there is no "ultimate criterion of accuracy," therefore choice 4 is correct.

53. Generally, the best ultrasonic testing method for detecting discontinuities oriented along the fusion zone in a welded plate is

1. an angle-beam contact method employing surface waves.

2. a contact test using a straight longitudinal wave.

3. an immersion test using surface waves.

4. an angle-beam method using shear waves.

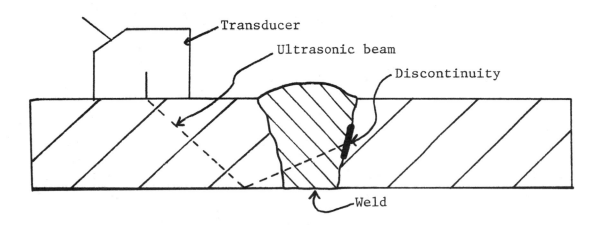

The fusion zone is the boundary between the weld filler metal and the base material being welded. A discontinuity located along this zone is <u>longitudinal</u> and <u>subsurface</u>, this rules out choices 1, 2, and 3. In practice, the angle beam method, illustrated above, is most often used. Choice 4 is correct.

An excellent reference on ultrasonic inspection is

Krautkrämer, J., <u>Ultrasonic Testing of Materials</u>, 2nd ed., Springer-Verlag, New York, 1968.

54. One of the practical limits on the application of
    ultrasonic testing methods is

    1. lack of portability.

    2. poor penetration capability.

    3. reference standards are required.

    4. inability to record results permanently.

Ultrasonic testing is extremely portable for an NDT method,
with excellent penetration capabilities. Recorders exist
that generate permanent inspection records (although these
records are not as widely accepted as X-Ray inspection film).
One limitation of ultrasonic methods is the need to calibrate
the equipment to detect a wide variety of flaws. Since different flaws produce different echo images and heights, it is
difficult to produce reliable standards. Choice 3 is correct.

55. Calibration intervals should be adjusted when

    1. no defective product is reported as acceptable
       due to measurement errors.

    2. few instruments are scrapped during calibration.

    3. the results of previous calibrations reflect few
       "out of tolerance" conditions during calibration.

    4. a particular characteristic on the gage is
       consistently found out of tolerance.

Of course, choice 4 describes a situation where the calibration interval should be shortened. The reader is again

referred to MIL-STD-45662 (see question #48 of this section).

    56. In selecting a base for measuring quality costs,

        which of the following should be considered?

        1. Is it sensitive to increases and decreases in

           production schedules?

        2. Is it affected by mechanization and the resulting

           lower direct labor costs?

        3. Is it affected by seasonal product sales?

        4. Is it oversensitive to material price fluctuations?

        5. All of the above.

The answer is number 5. One of the most widespread problems associated with any economic comparison of an indicator to a base is to determine whether an observed movement in the comparison index was due to a change in the indicator or a change in the base. Unfortunately, no easy formula exists to help you choose a base.

*   *   *

This is a good time to review the "Notes on Quality Costs" that are just after question 58 in the previous section. The answers to the next several questions are based on this material, and the reference material cited.

You can see from the number of questions that ASQC, rightly, considers cost analysis to be a vital area. The prospective CQE should take the time to read several reference sources on this subject before sitting for the CQE exam. An interesting series of articles is

Harrington, H.J., "Quality Costs--the whole and its parts (Parts I and II)," Quality, May-June 1976.

Sullivan, E. and Owens, D.A., "Catching a Glimpse of Quality Costs Today," Quality Progress, pp. 16-24, Dec. 1983.

*   *   *

57. For a typical month, 900D Manufacturing Company

identified and reported the following quality costs:

Inspection wages . . . . $ 12,000

Quality planning . . . . $ 4,000

Source inspection . . . . $ 2,000

In-plant scrap and rework . . . . $ 88,000

Final product test $110,000

Retest and troubleshooting . . . . $ 39,000

Field warranty cost $205,000

Evaluation and processing of

   deviation requests . . . . $ 6,000

What is the total failure cost for this month?

1. $244,000

2. $151,000

3. $261,000

4. $205,000

5. $332,000

The failure costs are

Item	Amount
In-plant scrap and rework	$ 88,000
Retest and troubleshooting	39,000
Field warranty cost	205,000
TOTAL	$332,000

Choice 5.

(NOTE: Evaluation and processing of deviation requests is
an appraisal cost.)

58. **Refer to previous question**

One year later, the monthly quality costs reported

by 900D Manufacturing Company were as follows:

Inspection wage . . . . $ 14,000

Quality planning . . . . $ 8,500

Source inspection . . . . $ 2,200

In-plant scrap and rework . . . . $ 51,000

Quality training . . . . $ 42,000

Audits . . . . $ 47,000

Final product test $103,000

Retest and troubleshooting . . . . $ 19,000

Field warranty cost $188,000

Evaluation & processing of

deviation requests . . . . $ 4,500

Sales billed have increased 10% from the corresponding

month of a year ago. How would you evaluate the

effectiveness of 900D quality improvement program?

1. Quality costs are still too high.

2. Essentially no change in overall results.

3. Good improvement.

4. Still further improvement is unlikely.

5. Not enough information to evaluate.

Total Quality Costs - Year 1: $466,000

Total Quality Costs - Year 2: $479,200

Change = +2.8%

If our only comparison base is sales billed, then the increase in quality costs is smaller than would be expected. Thus choice 3 is correct. Keep in mind, however, that in the real world cost analysis is far more complex, usually involving several bases and breakdown of costs into various categories.

59. If prevention costs are increased to pay for engineering work in quality control, and this results in a reduction in the number of product defects, this yields a reduction in

    1. appraisal costs.

    2. operating costs.

    3. quality costs.

    4. failure costs.

    5. manufacturing costs.

Referring to the discussion after question #58 in the previous section, we find that failure costs are defined as costs related to <u>defects</u>; choice 4 is most correct. This doesn't mean that the other costs listed won't change too, but the only costs we can be sure about are failure costs.

60. Analysis of quality costs consists of

    1. reviewing manpower utilization against standard.

    2. evaluating seasonal productivity.

    3. establishing management tools to determine net worth.

4. examining each cost element in relation to other elements and the total.

5. providing an accounting mechanism to spread costs over serviced areas.

The analysis of quality costs is described best by choice 4.

61. Assume that the cost data available to you for a certain period are limited to the following:

Final test . . . . $ 18,000
Loss on disposition of surplus stock . . . $ 15,000
Field warranty costs $275,000
Scrap $150,000
Customer returns . . . . $ 25,000
Planning for inspection . . . . $ 16,000

The total of the quality costs is:

1. $499,000.

2. $484,000.

3. $468,000.

4. $193,000.

Choice 2 is correct. Loss on disposition of surplus stock is not a quality cost.

62. Market based cost standards are guided by

1. what others spend.

2. what we ought to spend.

3. marketing budget.

4. quality analysis forecast.

116

Many, many companies base their expenditures on what others in similar circumstances spend. These are called "market base cost standards," choice 1. The quality profession is familiar with market based <u>quality</u> <u>standards</u>, where the quality of one's product is judged compared to the quality of competing product.

63. Historic levels of defects, with rare exceptions, have been found to be located at what point, with respect to the optimum point in the figure?

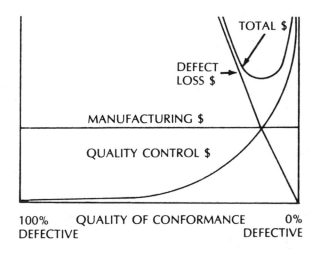

1. To the left of the optimum.

2. To the right of the optimum.

3. At the center of the optimum.

4. None of the above.

Historically, the defect rate has been higher than optimum, or to the left of optimum on the graph shown. Choice 1 is correct. The reasons that this has been are so many and varied as to be worth a book all their own (in fact, such best sellers as In Search of Excellence, Theory Z, and Japanese Manufacturing Techniques address this problem); a brief discussion is provided in the articles by Harrington cited above.

64. The cost of writing instructions and operating

    procedures for inspection and testing should be

    charged to

    1. prevention costs.

    2. appraisal costs.

    3. internal failure costs.

    4. external failure costs.

Choice 1 is correct, tricky eh? A natural tendency is to classify these costs as appraisal costs. However, a review of the reference material, including the definitions provided in this study guide, show clearly that these are prevention costs. Perhaps it is easier to understand if one considers the case where we are writing procedures for analyzing field failures. Obviously it would be absurd to call the cost of developing these procedures failure costs.

65. Which of the following activities is not normally

    charged as a preventive cost?

    1. Quality training.

    2. Design and development of quality measurement

       equipment.

3. Quality planning.

4. Laboratory acceptance testing.

Choice 4 describes an appraisal cost. Charges in this category would include work done, for example, by Underwriter's Laboratories.

*   *   *

Notes on Quality Audits

The next several questions relate to the important activity of quality audit. Like most subject areas, you won't be able to answer these questions by looking up the answer in some book. You must study the subject well enough beforehand to gain an understanding of it; this will help you reason through the questions to get the correct answer. The following references will help in this. In addition, you should, of course, read the sections in the Quality Control Handbook that relate to quality audit; these are given in the course outline in the appendix.

Quality Audit References

Van Dine, H.A., Jr., "Quality Auditing--Familiar Land Explored," Quality Progress, pp. 34-37, Nov. 1978.

Wachniak, R., "Ten Commandments for Quality Auditors," Quality, pp. 36-37, Nov. 1979.

Butler, E.S., "Effective Quality Assurance Audits," Quality Progress, pp. 22-24, Jan. 1980.

*   *   *

66. A quality audit program should begin with

1. a study of the quality documentation system.

2. an evaluation of the work being performed.

3. a report listing findings, the action taken,
   and recommendations.

4. a charter of policy, objectives, and procedures.

5. a follow-up check on the manager's response to
   recommendations.

The key word here is begin. Choice 4 describes activities
that occur at the start of a quality audit program. The
other choices describe actual audit activities.

67. Auditing of a quality program is most effective on a

1. quarterly basis, auditing all characteristics on
   the checklist.

2. periodic unscheduled basis, auditing some of the
   procedures.

3. monthly basis, auditing selected procedures.

4. continuing basis, auditing randomly selected
   procedures.

5. continually specified time period basis, frequency
   adjustable, auditing randomly selected procedures.

The basics of quality audit scheduling and subject matter are
thoroughly described in the above references, and in section
21 of the Quality Control Handbook (see especially pp. 21-6
to 21-11). The correct choice is 5.

68. An inspection performance audit is made of
eight inspectors in an area of complex assembly,
all doing similar work. Seven inspectors have
an average monthly acceptance rate of 86 to 92%;
one inspector has an average rate of 72% with
approximately four times the daily variation as
the others. As inspection supervisor you should,
based on this audit,

1. promote the 72% inspector as he is very
   conscientious.

2. discipline the 72% inspector as he is creating
   needless rework and wasted time.

3. initiate a special investigation of inspection
   and manufacturing performance.

4. discipline the other seven inspectors as they
   are not "cracking down."

The audit result indicates only that a problem exists, it
tells us nothing about the cause of the problem. Choices 1,
2, and 4 all presume information that was not given. The
difference could be in the training, gaging, lighting, or
any number of other things. Only choice 3 is reasonable.

69. The quality audit could be used to judge all of
the following except

1. a prospective vendor's capability for meeting
   quality standards.

    2. the adequacy of a current vendor's system for controlling quality.

    3. the application of a specification to a unique situation.

    4. the adequacy of a company's own system for controlling quality.

Choice 3 is clearly <u>not</u> an appropriate activity for a quality audit. If this is not immediately obvious, you should re-read the reference materials.

    70. Audit inspectors should report to someone who is independent from

    1. middle management.

    2. marketing.

    3. inspection supervision.

    4. production staff.

One of the guiding principles of quality audit is that they are carried out by trained or experienced persons who are independent, i.e. they have no responsibility for the conduct of the activity being audited. This principle makes choice 3 correct.

    71. When requesting "worst case" design analysis, you expect the Reliability Group to

    1. analyze the worst rejects.

    2. analyze only those products failing to meet

specification requirements.

3. determine whether product requirements can be met with subassemblies assumed at their worst combination of tolerances.

4. assume all subassembly tolerances at their maximum limit.

Choice 3 describes worst case analysis. Worst case analysis is the traditional approach to tolerance evaluation. The modern approach also considers the <u>probabilities</u> associated with these "events" (e.g. an "event" is that two or more sub-assemblies are at their maximum tolerances).

72. For a high compression aircraft air conditioning system, the MTBF is 100 hours. This mean life is allocated to four serial units comprising the total system. The unit failure rates are then weighted as follows:

$$W_1 = 0.1250 \qquad W_3 = 0.1875$$
$$W_2 = 0.2500 \qquad W_4 = 0.4375$$

Based upon the above data, indicate which of the following is the correct calculation for one of the units.

1. $\lambda_3 = 0.0018750$

2. $\lambda_4 = 0.0435700$

3. $\lambda_1 = 0.0125000$

4. $\lambda_3 = 0.0001875$

5. $\lambda_2 = 0.0025100$

A system with four serial units can be representated as follows:

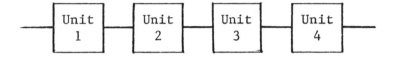

In such a system all four units must function or the system will fail. The reliability of this system can be easily determined as

$$R_s = R_1 \times R_2 \times R_3 \times R_4$$

where R_s = System reliability

R_1 = Unit 1 reliability

etc.

In words, the reliability of the system is the product of the unit reliabilities. If we can assume constant and independent failure rates, then

$$\lambda_s = \frac{1}{MTBF} = \frac{1}{\lambda_1 + \lambda_2 + \lambda_3 + \lambda_4}$$

where λ_s = The system failure rate

λ_1 = Unit 1 failure rate

etc.

Relative unit weights are found using

$$W_j = \frac{\lambda_j}{\lambda_s}$$

Thus $\qquad \lambda_j = W_j \lambda_s \quad$ or $\quad \lambda_j = W_j/100$

So $\qquad \lambda_1 = .00125 \quad ; \quad \lambda_2 = .00250$

$\qquad \lambda_3 = .001875 \quad ; \quad \lambda_4 = .004375$

The only correct choice is choice 1.

73. What is the reliability of a system at 850 hours, if the average usage on the system was 400 hours for 1650 items and the total number of failures was 145? Assume an exponential distribution.

1. 0%

2. 36%

3. 18%

4. 83%

Using the exponential

$$R_s = e^{-t/MTBF}$$

where R_s = System reliability at time t.

t = Operating time

MTBF = Mean time between failure

e = 2.71828...

The MTBF is

$$MTBF = \frac{Time \times Units}{Failures} = \frac{400 \times 1650}{145} = 4552 \text{ hours}$$

$$R_s = e^{-850/4552} = 83\%$$

Choice 4.

74. The probability of an accident for the head event

   "H" given below is

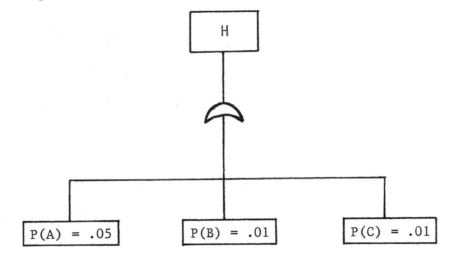

   1. .1125

   2. .0689

   3. .1100

   4. None of the above.

An accident will occur if event A <u>OR</u> B <u>OR</u> C recur. From
probability theory we know that

$$P(A \cup B \cup C) = P(A) + P(B) + P(C) - P(A \cap B)$$
$$- P(A \cap C) - P(B \cap C) + P(A \cap B \cap C)$$

So $P(H) = .05 + .01 + .01 - (.05)(.01) - (.05)(.01)$
$$- (.01)(.01) + (.05)(.01)(.01)$$
$$= .068905$$

Choice 2.

   75. A reliability data system usually implies collecting

      data on

126

1. process machine downtime.

2. product failures and operating time.

3. maintenance costs.

4. repair times.

Most reliability data systems, such as GIDEP, collect data on product failures and operating times, choice 2. The usefulness of this data was demonstrated in question #73.

76. In consumer products, the complaint rate is most

directly a measure of

1. product quality.

2. customer satisfaction.

3. market value.

4. rejection rate.

5. specification conformance.

The key words are "most directly." Choice 2 is most directly measured by the customer complaint rate.

77. Quality data, which are regularly obtained but

not used, should be

1. analyzed periodically by an expert statistician

to glean as much information as possible.

2. discontinued to save time and money.

3. stored until such time as the need arises.

4. processed by computer and summary reports issued

regularly to interested persons.

Some organizations spend huge sums of money handling quality data that is never used. If the data are truly important, it is unlikely that this would occur "regularly." Useless data is uselses even if analyzed by a statistician or processed by a computer or saved; the famous "garbage in garbage out" syndrome. The best choice is #2.

78. Primary personal characteristics, for reliable

inspector performance evaluation, are

1. experience and amount of time of observed

performance.

2. relevancy, consistency and lack of bias.

3. personal appearance, mental alertness and

ability to communicate.

4. seniority, age and good health.

5. All of the above.

While I am not sure what "relevancy" is as a "personal char-acteristic," choice 2 is clearly the best of the lot. Consistency and lack of bias are vitally important to reli-able inspector performance.

79. An essential technique in making training programs

effective is to

1. set group goals.

2. have training classes which teach skills and

knowledge required.

3. feed back to the employee meaningful measures
of his performance.

4. post results of performance before and after
the training program.

5. set individual goals instead of group goals.

The only choice that is truly essential to effective training is #3. One could debate choices 1 or 5, and choice 5 might even be counterproductive. Choice 2 implies that effective training requires classroom teaching, which isn't necessarily true.

80. A method of dealing with an inspector, found to
be falsifying the results of inspection of
borderline product, is to

1. criticize the inspector on the basis that the
pattern of reading does not follow the laws
of chance.

2. review the procedure for evaluating and reporting
borderline product.

3. review the inspector's results against the
expected results calculated from a normal curve.

4. criticize the inspector for not knowing how to
read the inspection equipment.

After having spent several years as an inspector for various companies, you can take it from me: procedures for evaluating and reporting borderline product, if they even exist, are often woefully inadequate. Choice 2 is an excellent place to begin the study of the problem described.

APPENDIX

I.   Certified Quality Engineer fact sheet.............. 131

II.   Quality Engineer in Training (QEIT) fact sheet 132

III.   CQE refresher course outline and syllabus
(QC Handbook version) 133

IV.   CQE refresher course outline and syllabus
(Quality Planning and Analysis version) 136

V.   CQE refresher course quizzes 139

VI.   Answers to quizzes 157

VII.   CQE refresher course final exam 158

VIII. Final exam answers 174

IX.   CQE exams published in Quality Progress magazine .. 175

X.   ASQC certification program booklet 195

CERTIFIED QUALITY ENGINEER

Quality engineering is that speciality branch of professional engineering which requires such education and experience as to master the unique body of knowledge of substantial intellectual content which makes up the quality sciences and to understand and apply the principles of product and service quality evaluation and control. This body of knowledge and applied technologies include, but are not limited to: development and operation of quality control systems; application and analysis of testing and inspection procedures; the ability to apply metrology and statistical methods to diagnose and correct improper quality control practices to assure product and service conformity to prescribed standards; an understanding of human factors and motivation; facility with quality cost concepts and techniques; and the knowledge and ability to develop and administer management information systems and audit of quality systems for deficiency identification and correction.

Qualifications for Certified Quality Engineer

On the job experience in the Quality Sciences is a requirement for Certification.

A. Eight years of experience in the Quality Sciences, three of which must be in a decision making position as a Quality Engineer.

B. Completed educational degrees in Quality Technology, Engineering, Mathematics, the Basic Sciences or related fields, from colleges or universities with accreditation satisfactory to ASQC will waive the following Quality Science experience requirements.

   1. Masters Degree - Five years
   2. Bachelors Degree - Four years
   3. Associate Degree - Two years
   4. Certificate for a Quality Technology program from a Community College or Vocational School - One year

Body of Knowledge

Fundamentals of Probability, Statistical Quality Control and Design of Experiments; Quality Planning, Management and Product Liability; Metrology, Inspection and Testing; Quality Cost Analysis; Quality Auditing; Reliability, Maintainability and Product Safety; Quality Information Systems; Human Factors and Motivation.

QUALITY ENGINEER-IN-TRAINING

A. The candidate must have a completed bachelor's degree in either Quality Technology, Engineering, Mathematics, the Basic Sciences or related fields from colleges or universities with accreditation satisfactory to ASQC.

B. Proof of Professionalism. Evidence of professionalism must be presented by one of these means.
   1. Current member of ASQC evidenced by:
      a. Photostat of current membership card, or
      b. Photostat of welcoming letter, or
      c. Submission of completed, or membership application with proper fee.
   OR 2. Current membership of another professional society, which is itself a member of either the American Association of Engineering Societies or the Accreditation Board for Engineering and Technology, Inc., evidenced by:
      a. Photostat of your membership card, or
      b. Photostat of your certificate.
   OR 3. To verify professionalism, provide two signatures of persons who are members of ASQC or any other Society belonging to the American Association of Engineering Societies or the Accreditation Board for Engineering and Technology, Inc., or a related engineering society of stature, subject to the discretion of the ASQC Certification Committee.
   OR 4. Registered Professional Engineer evidenced by:
      a. Photostat of your membership card, or
      b. Photostat of your certificate.

C. The candidate must pass the Principles portion of the CQE examination to be recnized as a Quality-Engineer-In-Training.

D. Upon completion of the MINIMUM experience requirement, the QE-In-Training may take the applications portion of the CQE examination to become a CQE.

EDUCATION	MINIMUM EXPERIENCE
Bachelor's Degree	4 years
Master's Degree	3 years
Ph.D.	3 years

The Quality Engineer-In-Training program must be completed within six years of the Quality Engineer-In-Training award.

E. Applicants who do not meet the requirement in (A) above will not be eligible for the Engineer-In-Training status.

F. Full CQE application and examination fees must be paid upon initial application to the QE-In-Training program. All other appropriated fees (i.e. retake, absence and unqualified funds) will apply.

QUALITY CONTROL CERTIFICATION REFRESHER
COURSE OUTLINE AND SYLLABUS
QC HANDBOOK VERSION

Course Objectives

To prepare qualified students for the ASQC Certified Quality Engineering (CQE) examination by reviewing the body of knowledge of quality control engineering.

Text & Materials

Quality Control Handbook, fourth edition, J.M. Juran, ed., McGraw Hill, New York, 1988

Grading

Quizzes: There will be 8 in-class quizzes administered. Most quizzes will contain 10 multiple choice questions. You will be given 20 minutes to complete the quiz, approximately the same time per question as in the real CQE exam. The questions may cover any of the previous material. Quizzes will all be open books, notes, calculators, or anything else you want to open. No reference material is allowed that contains questions or answers from previous CQE exams. 60% of your course grade will be based on the quizzes.

Final exam: The final exam will be comprehensive and will consist of two parts, each timed and graded separately. The final will also be open book notes, etc. 40% of your course grade will be based on the final exam. Allow 1 hour and 15 minutes for each part.

CQE REFRESHER COURSE SYLLABUS

QC HANDBOOK, 4th EDITION VERSION

Session #1   Quality from the customer's viewpoint, basic concepts of quality control. Reading: Sections 1, 2, 3, 5 and 20.

Session #2   QUIZ #1. Vendor quality control concepts, quality costs, Pareto analysis. Reading: sections 4, 15, 22.19 to 22.36.

Session #3   QUIZ #2. Human factors, process control concepts, inspection and test concepts. Reading: sections 12, 16.9 to 16.37, 18.

Session #4   QUIZ #3. Quality organization, quality information systems, quality audit. Reading: 6.40 to 6.45, 7, 9.5 to 9.14, 27.

Session #5   QUIZ #4. Probability, enumeration, discrete probability distributions. Reading: 23.1 to 23.32.

Session #6   Histograms, continuous distributions, probability plotting. Reading: 23.32 to 23.45.

Session #7   QUIZ #5. Confidence limits, statistical inference. Reading: 23.45 to 23.60.

Session #8   Hypothesis testing, OC curves for tests of hypotheses. Reading: 23.60 to 23.81.

Session #9   QUIZ #6. Statistical process control. Reading: 24.

Session #10   Design of experiments. Reading: 26.1 to 26.29.

Session #11   QUIZ #7. Design of experiments (continued), regression analysis. Reading: 23.96, 23.118, 26.36 to 26.77.

Session #12   Acceptance sampling. Reading: 25.

Session #13   QUIZ #8. Designing for reliability.
               Reading: 13.17 to 13.55, 14, 23.81 to
               23.91.

Session #14   Measurement, warranty, product
               liability. Reading: 18.57 to 18.97,
               19.8 to 19.18.

Session #15   Final exam. Part I: PRINCIPLES, Part
               II: APPLICATIONS. Allow exactly 1 hour
               and 15 minutes for each part, take a
               short break between each part. The exam
               is open book and notes but **NO SHARING
               WITH NEIGHBORS AND NO MATERIALS THAT
               INCLUDE OLD CQE EXAM QUESTIONS!** This is
               your "dress rehearsal" for the real CQE
               exam so try to prepare for it just as
               you would for the actual exam. Bring
               all the materials and references you
               expect to need at the actual exam. If
               you find that some needed material is
               missing, make a note of it so you will
               be ready when you take the CQE exam.

               Good luck!

Quality Control Certification Refresher

Recommended Course for Classroom or Self-Study
Based on the text
WHAT EVERY ENGINEER SHOULD KNOW ABOUT QUALITY CONTROL

Course Objectives

To prepare qualified students for the ASQC Certified Quality Engineering examination by reviewing the body of knowledge of quality engineering. The course consists of fifteen sessions of two hours and thirty minutes each (equivalent to a three credit hour course).

Texts & materials

Pyzdek, T. (1989), What Every Engineer Should Know About Quality Control, Marcel Dekker (New York) and ASQC Quality Press (Milwaukee, WI), 1989. ISBN 0-8247-7966-5, 251 pages, hardcover, $49.75 (USA, Canada), $59.50 (all other countries).

Pyzdek, T. (1990), CQE Examination Study Guide, Quality Publishing, Inc., Tucson, Arizona. ISBN 0-930011-01-5, 240 pages, softcover, $34.95.

Both titles are available from Quality Publishing, Inc. 1-800-628-0432. You will be billed $5 per order shipping and handling, or actual freight charges, whichever is higher. Visa, Mastercard, American Express or company purchase orders accepted.

Grading

Eight quizzes are provided in the CQE Examination Study Guide. You should allow yourself twenty minutes to complete each quiz. A two-part final exam is also included. When taking the final exam, try to simulate the ASQC-CQE exam situation; i.e., open book, no old exam material allowed, etc.. You should allow yourself one hour and fifteen minutes for each part of the exam (the time-per-question is the same as you will have for the actual CQE exam).

NOTES

1. ASQC will not allow the CQE Examination Study Guide to be taken into the actual examination with you. However, you are allowed to take What Every Engineer Should Know About Quality Control with you. The same rule applies to your quizzes and the final exam.

2. At the end of each chapter in What Every Engineer Should Know About Quality Control is a discussion of additional subject material that should be mastered by anyone seeking an in-depth understanding of quality, recommended reading is also provided. As a CQE candidate, you should avail yourself of the additional materials in any areas where you feel weak.

CQE REFRESHER COURSE SYLLABUS
Based on the text
WHAT EVERY ENGINEER SHOULD KNOW ABOUT QUALITY CONTROL

Session #1   Basic concepts of quality control, product liability. Reading assignment: chapter 1 (all).

Session #2   **Quiz #1.** Vendor quality control concepts, quality costs, Pareto Analysis. Reading assignment: chapter 2 (all), pages 56 - 63, pages 115-118.

Session #3   **Quiz #2.** Motivation, process control concepts. Reading assignment: chapter 3 (all), pages 101 - 113.

Session #4   **Quiz #3.** Quality organization, quality information systems, and quality audit. Reading assignment: pages 43 - 56 and chapter 5 (all).

Session #5   **Quiz #4.** Probability, enumeration and discreet probability distributions. Reading assignment: pages 83 - 91.

Session #6   Histograms, continuous distributions. Reading assignment: pages 91 - 96, 119 - 121.

Session #7   **Quiz #5.** Confidence limits, hypothesis testing and statistical inference. Reading assignment: pages 96 - 100.

Session #8   SPC methods for discrete attributes data. Reading assignment: pages 127 - 137.

Session #9   **Quiz #6.** SPC methods for continuous variables data. Reading assignment: pages 121 - 127, 137 - 148.

Session #10   **Quiz #7.** Concepts of statistically designed experiments. Reading assignment: chapter 9 (all).

Session #11   Acceptance sampling. Reading assignment: chapter 8 (all).

Session #12   **Quiz #8.** Reliability concepts. Reading assignment: chapter 10 (all).

<u>Session #13</u>   Measurement error analysis. Reading assignment:
chapter 11 (all).

<u>Session #14</u>   Modern approaches to quality improvement. Reading
assignment: chapter 12 (all).

<u>Session #15</u>   **Final exam.** Part I: PRINCIPLES, Part II:
APPLICATIONS.

1. In planning for quality, an important consideration at the start is:

    1. the relation of the total cost of quality to the net sales.
    2. the establishment of a company quality policy or objective.
    3. deciding precisely how much money is to be spent.
    4. the selling of the quality program to top management.

2. Establishing the quality policy for the company is the responsibility of:

    1. customer.
    2. quality control.
    3. marketing department.
    4. top management.

3. In planning the staffing for your new quality control department, you use which of the following as the best justification for estimating the number of people required?

    1. a given ratio of production employees to quality personnel, typical of the industry.
    2. a total salary budget as a given percent of sales dollars.
    3. the number of people in the engineering department.
    4. the quality objectives that have been set by top management.
    5. none of the above.

4. When planning the specifications for product quality in the so-called "mechanical" industries:

    1. market research establishes economic tolerances.
    2. product design assumes prime responsibility for establishing economic tolerances.
    3. product research issues official product specifications.
    4. quality control develops products possessing qualities that meet consumer needs.
    5. all of the above.

5. In the planning of a new major manufacturing program, the greatest quality effort should be put logically in:

    1. inspection of product.
    2. nondestructive testing equipment.
    3. nonconformance to specifications.
    4. prevention of occurrence of substandard quality.

6. When planning quality control functions, which one of the following is most directly related to production of a quality product?

    1. process control and process capability.
    2. suitable blueprints.
    3. dimensional tolerancing.
    4. product audit.

7. When developing and implementing a modern quality assurance program, the perspective of which of the following disciplines is most useful?

    1. financial management.
    2. production control.
    3. accounting management.
    4. manufacturing engineering.
    5. systems engineering.

8. Two of the most fundamental aspects of product quality are:

    1. appraisal costs and failure costs.
    2. in-process and finished product quality.
    3. quality of design and quality of conformance.
    4. impact of machines and impact of men.
    5. none of these.

9. In the pre-production phase of quality planning, an appropriate activity would be to:

    1. determine responsibility for process control.
    2. determine the technical depth of available manpower.
    3. establish compatible approaches for accumulation of process data.
    4. conduct process capability studies to measure process expectations.

10. In preparing a Quality Policy concerning a product line for your company you should not:

    1. specify the means by which quality performance is measured.
    2. develop criteria for identifying risk situations, and specify whose approval is required when there are known risks.
    3. load the policy with procedural matters or ordinary functional responsibilities.
    4. identify responsibilities for dispositioning defective hardware.
    5. answers 2 and 4 above.

1. Communication with vendors on quality problems:
    1. should be initiated by the vendor's quality control department to the vendee's quality control department.
    2. should be initiated by the vendee's purchasing department and the vendor.
    3. should be initiated by the vendee's engineering department and the vendor.
    4. can be resolved <u>only</u> through personal visits between vendor and vendee.

2. When purchasing materials from vendors, it is sometimes advantageous to choose vendors whose prices are higher because:
    1. such a statement is basically incorrect; always buy at lowest bid price.
    2. such vendors may become obligated to bestow special favors.
    3. materials that cost more can be expected to be better, and "you get what you pay for."
    4. the true cost of purchased material, which should include items such as sorting inspection, contacting vendors and production delays, may be lower.

3. The primary reason for evaluating and maintaining surveillance over a supplier's quality program is to:
    1. perform product inspection at source.
    2. eliminate incoming inspection costs.
    3. improve human and customer relations and motivate suppliers in improving quality.
    4. make sure the supplier's quality program is accomplishing its intended functions effectively and economically.

4. When planning the quality aspects of packing and shipping, it is not usual that the:
    1. product design department specify packaging and shipping procedures.
    2. shipping department conduct packing and shipping operations.
    3. inspection department determine package specifications.
    4. inspection department check the adequacy of packing and shipping operations.

5. The most desirable method of evaluating a supplier is:

    1. history evaluation.
    2. survey evaluation.
    3. questionaire.
    4. discuss with quality manager on phone.
    5. all of the above.

6. Quality costs:

    1. are the total of all Quality Control costs.
    2. are not significant in governmental applications.
    3. are the sum of Quality Control costs and failure costs.
    4. all of the above.

7. Assume that the cost data available to you for a certain
   period are limited to the following:

       $ 20,000 - Final test
        350,000 - Field warranty costs
        170,000 - Reinspection and retest
         45,000 - Inventory reduction
          4,000 - Vendor quality surveys
         30,000 - Rework

The total of the quality costs is:

    1. $619,000
    2. $615,000
    3. $574,000
    4. $570,000

8. The percentages of total quality costs are distributed
   as follows:

       Prevention 2%
       Appraisal 33%
       Internal failure 35%
       External failure 30%

We can conclude:

    1. expenditures for failures are excessive.
    2. nothing.
    3. we should invest more money in prevention.
    4. the amount spent for appraisal seems about right.

9. This month's quality cost data collection shows the
   following:

   Adjustment of customer complaints . . . . $ 3,500
   Rework and repair   10,700
   Quality management salaries   25,000
   Downgrading expense   1,800
   Warranty replacement   53,500
   Calibration and maintenance of
       test equipment   2,500
   Inspection and testing   28,000

   For your "action" report to top management you select which
   one of the following as the percentage of "external failure" to total quality costs to show the true impact of
   field problems?

   1. 24%
   2. 65%
   3. 56%
   4. 46%

10. In analyzing the cost data below:

    $ 20,000 - Final test
      350,000 - Field warranty costs
      170,000 - Reinspection and retest
       45,000 - Loss or disposition of surplus stock
        4,000 - Vendor quality surveys
       30,000 - Rework

    We might conclude that:

    1. internal failure costs can be decreased.
    2. prevention cost is too low a proportion of the
       quality costs shown.
    3. appraisal costs should be increased.
    4. nothing can be concluded.

1. When planning the specifications for product quality in the so-called "mechanical" industries:

   1. market research establishes economic tolerances.
   2. product design assumes prime responsibility for establishing economic tolerances.
   3. product research issues official product specifications.
   4. quality control develops products possessing qualities that meet consumer needs.
   5. all of the above.

2. When developing and implementing a modern quality assurance program, the perspective of which of the following disciplines is most useful?

   1. financial management.
   2. production control.
   3. accounting management.
   4. manufacturing engineering.
   5. systems engineering.

3. Quality cost data would not normally be obtained from which of the following?

   1. labor reports.
   2. capital expenditure reports.
   3. salary budget reports.
   4. scrap reports.
   5. any of these.

4. One of the most important techniques in making a training program effective is to:

   1. concentrate only on developing knowledge and skills needed to do a good job.
   2. transmit all of the information that is even remotely related to the function.
   3. set individual goals instead of group goals.
   4. give people meaningful measures of performance.

5. The most important activity of a material review board (MRB) would normally be:

   1. making sure that corrective action is taken to prevent recurrence of the problem.
   2. to provide a bonded or segregated area of holding discrepant material pending disposition.
   3. prepare discrepant material reports for management.
   4. accept discrepant material when "commercial" decisions dictate.
   5. none of the above.

6. One human management approach, often called the "carrot and the stick" approach is best typified by which of the following theories?

    1. Herzberg's "hygiene theory."
    2. Maslow's "hierarchy of motivation."
    3. Skinner's "reinforcement of behavior theory."
    4. McGregor's "theory X."

7. McGregor's theory X manager is typified as one who operates from the following basic assumption about people working for him (select the one best answer):

    1. performance can be improved through tolerance and trust.
    2. people have a basic need to produce.
    3. status is more important than money.
    4. self-actualization is the highest order of human need.
    5. people are lazy and are motivated by reward and punishment.

8. When installing a new system for collecting failure data in a manufacturing plant, the following approach is recommended:

    1. issue a procedure written by a quality engineer without help from other departments to prevent a biased input from production test technicians.
    2. have production write their own procedure.
    3. use a procedure from another company.
    4. enlist the collaboration of all affected departments in drafting and approving the procedure.
    5. none of the above.

9. Having designed a test fixture to performance requirements, the design should be carefully evaluated by the quality engineer to insure that it has included:

    1. low cost components.
    2. printout capability.
    3. human motor coordination factors.
    4. mass production methods.
    5. computer inputs.

10. In a visual inspection situation, one of the best ways to minimize deterioration of the quality level is to:

    1. re-train the inspector frequently.
    2. add variety to the task.
    3. have a program of frequent eye exams.
    4. have frequent breaks.
    5. have a standard to compare against a part of the operation.

1. Communication with vendors on quality problems:

    1. should be initiated by the vendor's quality control department to the vendee's quality control department.
    2. should be initiated by the vendee's purchasing department and the vendor.
    3. should be initiated by the vendee's engineering department and the vendor.
    4. can be resolved <u>only</u> through personal visits between vendor and vendee.

2. When planning a system for processing quality data or for keeping inspection and other quality records, the first step should be to:

    1. depict the system in a flow chart.
    2. hire a statistician.
    3. investigate applicable data processing equipment.
    4. determine the cost of operating the system.

3. In the so-called "process" industries:

    1. quality control has some responsibility in choosing the process.
    2. process development issues process specifications.
    3. quality control may help to establish process tolerances.
    4. all of the above.

4. Product characteristics should be classified (critical, major, etc.) so that:

    1. a more meaningful assessment of quality can be made.
    2. emphasis can be placed on important characteristics.
    3. action with the responsible individuals can be taken.
    4. a quality audit would be more meaningful.
    5. none of the above.

5. Which of the following elements is least necessary to a good corrective action feedback report?

    1. what caused the failure.
    2. who caused the failure.
    3. what correction has been made.
    4. when the correction is effective.
    5. how the corrected product is identified.

6. Data are:

    1. coded test/inspection measurements
    2. computer prepared summaries.
    3. collected raw facts.
    4. the output after processing that management wishes to know.

7. The primary responsibility for follow-up on corrective action commitments after an audit report usually rests with:

    1. production management.
    2. quality engineering.
    3. the function being audited.
    4. the audit group.

8. A shipping line product audit will directly measure:

    1. the outgoing product quality.
    2. the quality capability of production.
    3. the adequacy of inspection methods.
    4. the motivational level of the operators.

9. When selecting an audit sample size, which of the following rules should govern your choice?

    1. Since quality may change over time, we should look at a fixed quantity each time period for audit purposes.
    2. We need only a very small sample for audit purposes, as long as it is chosen at random.
    3. Any sample size if randomly selected can be suitable for audit purposes, since we are not directly performing lot acceptance or rejection.
    4. MIL-STD-105D is a scientific sampling procedure and we need scientific sampling for audit purposes.
    5. In general, ten percent is a good sample size to use. Also, it is easy to remember.

10. You are requested by top management to establish an audit program of the quality systems in each branch plant of your firm. Which of the following schemes would you use in selecting the audit team to optimize continuity, direction, availability, and technology transfer?

    1. full time audit staff.
    2. all volunteer audit staff.
    3. the boss' son and son-in-law.
    4. hybrid audit staff (a proportion of answers 1 and 2 above).
    5. any of the above will make an effective audit team.

1. The primary responsibility for follow-up on corrective action commitments after an audit report usually rests with:

    1. production management.
    2. quality engineering.
    3. the function being audited.
    4. the audit group.

2. You are requested by top management to establish an audit program of the quality systems in each branch plant of your firm. Which of the following schemes would you use in selecting the audit team to optimize continuity, direction, availability, and technology transfer?

    1. full time audit staff.
    2. all volunteer audit staff.
    3. the boss' son and son-in-law.
    4. hybrid audit staff (a proportion of answers 1 and 2 above).
    5. any of the above will make an effective audit team.

3. When planning a total quality system, one key objective is to provide a means of guaranteeing "the maintenance of product integrity." Which of the following quality system provisions is designed to most directly provide such a guarantee?

    1. drawing and print control.
    2. special process control.
    3. calibration and maintenance of test equipment.
    4. identification and segregation of nonconforming material.
    5. specification change control.

4. Quality motivation in industry should be directed at:

    1. manufacturing management.
    2. procurement and engineering.
    3. the quality assurance staff.
    4. the working force.
    5. all of the above.

5. The best reason for increased investment in quality information equipment (QIE) is that it will improve the total quality system by:

    1. providing better data collection.
    2. reducing the time span in the corrective action feedback loop.
    3. providing better information retrieval.
    4. reducing the paper work load of the QC department.

6. Suppose that you are blindfolded and five items are placed before you which are either defective or nondefective. The probability that you will identify all items correctly is approximately:

   1. 1.00
   2. 0.17
   3. 0.20
   4. 0.50
   5. 0.03

7. If the probability of success on a single trial is 0.3, and two trials are performed, what is the probability of at least one success?

   1. 0.910
   2. 0.410
   3. 0.510
   4. 0.490
   5. 0.030

8. Suppose that 5 bad electron tubes get mixed up with 8 good tubes. If 2 tubes are drawn simultaneously, what is the probability that both are good?

   1. 8/13
   2. 14/39
   3. 7/12
   4. 7/13
   5. 36/91

9. Complete examination of a small sample of finished product is characteristic of:

   1. final inspection.
   2. work sampling.
   3. process audit.
   4. product audit.

10. The quality cost of writing instructions and operating procedures for inspection and testing should be charged to:

    1. prevention costs.
    2. appraisal costs.
    3. internal failure costs.
    4. external failure costs.

** BONUS QUESTION (do only if you have spare time): Assume you guessed the answers to each of the above 10 questions, what is the probability that you scored 100%?

1. Human factors engineering concepts introduced to your final inspection area:

    1. are not valuable until the test equipment has been set up and operating.
    2. should be incorporated during the design and planning stage of the area.
    3. will result in schedules slippage wherever incorporated.
    4. are most costly when introduced during the design and planning stage of the area.
    5. will result in reduced efficiency of your inspectors, but greater accuracy.

2. What piece of data processing equipment can facilitate the handling of common quality control calculations on EDP equipment?

    1. Boolean algebra translator.
    2. collator.
    3. matrix inverter.
    4. tensor analyzer.

3. Calculate the standard deviation of the following set of population data: 11,7,12,10,8

    1. 4.3
    2. 2.2
    3. 1.9
    4. 5.0

4. When finding a confidence interval for the mean based on a sample size of n:

    1. increasing n increases the length of the confidence interval.
    2. having to use S_x instead of n decreases the length of the interval.
    3. the longer the interval, the better the estimate of the mean.
    4. increasing n decreases the length of the interval.

5. A process is producing material which is 40 percent defective. Four pieces are selected at random for inspection. What is the probability of exactly one defective being found in the sample?

    1. 0.870
    2. 0.575
    3. 0.346
    4. 0.130

6. Given $Z_{.05} = \pm 1.96$, the mean of a sample as 30 and the standard error of the mean as 5, the lower limit of the interval that would include the population mean with probability 0.95 is:

    1. 20.20
    2. 28.04
    3. 15.31
    4. 25.00
    5. 24.00

7. The lengths of a certain bushing are normally distributed with mean X'. How many standard deviation units, symmetrical about X', will include 70 percent of the lengths?

    1. ±1.04
    2. ±0.52
    3. ±1.28
    4. ±0.84

8. In determining a process average fraction defective using inductive or inferential statistics, we are making inferences about _____ based on _____ taken from the _____ .

    1. statistics, samples, populations
    2. populations, samples, populations
    3. samples, statistics, populations
    4. samples, populations, samples
    5. statistics, populations, statistics

9. A parameter is:

    1. a random variable.
    2. a sample value.
    3. a population value.
    4. the solution to a statistical problem.

10. The mean of either a discrete or a continuous distribution can always be visualized as:

    1. the point where 50% of the values are to the right side and 50% are to the left side.
    2. its center of gravity.
    3. the point where most of the values occur.
    4. all of the above.

152

1. Quality cost analysis has shown that appraisal costs are apparently too high in relation to sales. Which of the following actions probably would not be considered in pursuing this problem?

    1. work sampling in inspection and test areas.
    2. adding inspectors to reduce scrap costs.
    3. pareto analysis of quality costs.
    4. considering elimination of some test operations.
    5. comparing appraisal costs to bases other than sales-- for example, direct labor, added value, etc.

2. On the production floor, parts being produced measure .992-1.011. The specification requires the parts to be .995-1.005. Which of the following techniques would not be particularly useful in trying to improve and control the process?

    1. pre-control.
    2. MIL-STD-105 charts.
    3. Multi-vari charts.
    4. XBAR & R charts.
    5. machine capability analysis.

3. An XBAR and R chart was prepared for an operation using twenty samples with five pieces in each sample. XBAR was found to be 33.6 and RBAR was 6.2. During production a sample of five was taken and the pieces measured 36, 43, 37, 34 and 38. At the time this sample was taken:

    1. both average and range were within control limits.
    2. neither average nor range was within control limits.
    3. only the average was outside control limits.
    4. only the range was outside control limits.
    5. the information given is not sufficient to construct an XBAR and R chart using tables usually available.

4. Large panes of glass contain on the average 0.25 flaws per pane. The standard deviation of the distribution of flaws per pane is:
    1. 0.25
    2. 0.05
    3. 0.50
    4. 0.75
    5. none of the above

5. Which of the following techniques would not be used in a quality audit?

    1. select samples only from completed lots.
    2. examine samples from viewpoint of critical customer.
    3. audit only those items which have caused customer complaints.
    4. use audit information in future design planning.
    5. frequency of audit to depend on economic and quality requirements.

6. Match the following:

OBJECTIVE	TECHNIQUE
1. evaluate the defect rate on a complex electronic assembly on an ongoing basis	a. XBAR & R charts
2. sample from a small lot purchased from a distributor	b. p charts
	c. np charts
3. determine if two products have the same variance	d. Chi-square test
4. determine if the average performance of two machines is the same	e. F-test
5. control a process by counting the number of pieces in a sample that don't meet the color standard	f. poisson distribution
	g. hypergeometric distribution
6. control a process by measuring flatness	h. binomial distribution
7. determine if our inspection measurements are the same as those of our supplier on an important part	i. pascal distribution
	j. rayleigh distribution
	k. probability paper
8. determine the probability that a given sample result, measured in fraction defective, would be obtained from a controlled process	l. ANOVA
	m. t-test
9. determine the probability that a given sample result, measured in defects, would be obtained from a controlled process	n. c-charts
10. predict the yield based on a sample	

1. An effective report should have the following characteristics:

    1. the data and information are intermixed within the
       body of the report.
    2. the report is widely distributed.
    3. charts are never used.
    4. the data are compared with standards of performance
       which have previously been established.
    5. all of the above.

2. The famous Hawthorne study provided which of the following
   clinical evidence regarding the factors that can increase
   work group productivity?

    1. attention and recognition is more important than work-
       ing conditions.
    2. productivity did not change significantly under any
       of the test conditions.
    3. informal group pressures set a production "goal."
    4. people with higher capabilities are bored with routine
       jobs.
    5. work station layout is critical to higher produc-
       tivity.

3. The basic steps in any data processing system using computers generally are arranged in which of the following
   orders:

    1. data input, storage and retrieval, processing and
       output.
    2. collection, analysis, input, and output.
    3. evaluation, keypunch, processing and output.
    4. recording, input, calculation and output.
    5. keypunch, FORTRAN programming, output.

4. Given the following pairs of values of X and Y, what is
   the first step in determining if there is a linear association between X and Y?

$$X : 2, 4, 5, 5$$
$$Y : 6, 7, 4, 2$$

    1. draw a scatter diagram.
    2. calculate sums of squares.
    3. calculate correlation coefficient r.
    4. do nothing, get more data.

5. Estimate the biased variance of the population from which the following sample data came: 22, 18, 17, 20, 21

    1. 1.9
    2. 5.4
    3. 3.4
    4. 4.3

6. You have just conducted a designed experiment at three levels A, B, and C yielding the following "coded" data:

        A : 6,3,5,2
        B : 5,9,1
        C : 3,4,2

As a major step in your analysis you calculate the degrees of freedom for the "error" sum of squares to be:

    1. 7
    2. 9
    3. 3
    4. 2
    5. 10

7. A 3^2 experiment indicates:

    1. two levels of three factors.
    2. three independent variables and two dependent variables.
    3. three levels of two factors.
    4. two go/no-go variables and three continous variables.

8. Find the predicted system reliability for the three parts shown if the individual part reliability is 90% each for a specified mission time and mission conditions:

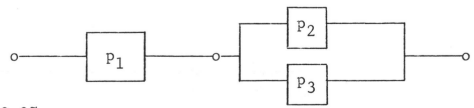

    1. 72.9%
    2. 70.0%
    3. 99.9%
    4. 89.1%
    5. 90.0%

9. Parts in use during the "wearout" portion of the part life cycle curve will exhibit:

    1. a constant failure rate.
    2. a decreasing failure rate.
    3. a low failure rate.
    4. an increasing failure rate.

10. MIL-STD-105D sampling tables and procedures have the fundamental principle of providing:

    1. low probability of acceptance of poor product.
    2. high probability of acceptance of good product.
    3. low probability of acceptance of good product.
    4. high probability of acceptance of poor product.

ANSWERS TO QUIZZES

QUIZ # 1

Question	Answer
1	2
2	4
3	4
4	2
5	4
6	1
7	5
8	3
9	2
10	3

QUIZ # 2

Question	Answer
1	2
2	4
3	4
4	3
5	1
6	3
7	3
8	2
9	4
10	2

QUIZ #3

Question	Answer
1	2
2	5
3	2
4	4
5	1
6	4
7	5
8	4
9	3
10	5

QUIZ # 4

Question	Answer
1	2
2	1
3	4
4	2
5	2
6	3
7	4
8	1
9	3
10	4

QUIZ # 5

Question	Answer
1	4
2	4
3	4
4	5
5	2
6	5
7	3
8	2
9	4
10	1

QUIZ # 6

Question	Answer
1	2
2	2
3	3
4	4
5	3
6	1
7	1
8	2
9	3
10	2

QUIZ # 7

Question	Answer
1	2
2	2
3	3
4	3
5	3

6	OBJ.	TECH.
1		n
2		g
3		e
4		m
5		c
6		a
7		m
8		h
9		f
10		k

QUIZ # 8

Question	Answer
1	4
2	1
3	1
4	1
5	3
6	1
7	3
8	4
9	4
10	2

CQE REFRESHER COURSE
FINAL EXAM

PART I: PRINCIPLES

1. Complete examination of a small sample of finished product is characteristic of:
   1. final inspection.
   2. work sampling.
   3. process audit.
   4. product audit.

2. Quality cost data:
   1. must be maintained when the end product is for the government.
   2. must be mailed to the contracting officer on request.
   3. is often an effective means of identifying quality problem areas.
   4. all of the above.

3. A thorough analysis of the cause and effect of plant quality problems usually indicates that a major percentage of the basic factors effecting poor quality performance are:
   1. operator controllable.
   2. management controllable.
   3. union controllable.
   4. customer controllable.
   5. none of the above.

4. Which of the following is most important to consider when calibrating a piece of equipment?
   1. calibration sticker.
   2. maintenance history card.
   3. wheatstone bridge.
   4. standard used.
   5. calibration interval.

5. A p-chart has exhibited statistical control over a period of time. However, the average fraction defective is too high to be satisfactory. Improvement can be obtained by:
   1. a change in the basic design of the product.
   2. instituting 100% inspection.
   3. a change in the production process through substitution of new tooling or machinery.
   4. all of the above answers are correct except number 2.
   5. all of the above are correct except number 3.

6. In linear measurement, what overriding consideration should guide the quality control engineer in specifying the measuring instrument to be used?
    1. the ability of the instrument to be read to one decimal place beyond that of the base dimension to be measured.
    2. the ability of the instrument to meet the error rule-of-thumb.
    3. the ability of the inspector-instrument system to obtain the necessary accurate data at a minimum overall cost.
    4. the combination of base dimension and tolerance in relation to measurement error.
    5. the ability of the inspector to use the measuring instrument.

7. A p-chart is a type of control chart for:
    1. plotting bar-stock lengths from receiving inspection samples.
    2. plotting fraction defective results from shipping inspection samples.
    3. plotting defects per unit from in-process inspection samples.
    4. answers 1,2, and 3 above.
    5. answers 1 and 3 only.

8. A very useful attribute control chart for plotting the actual number of defects found during an inspection is known as the:
    1. x-bar and r chart.
    2. np chart.
    3. p chart.
    4. c chart.
    5. u chart.

9. Which of the following is not a legitimate audit function?
    1. identify function responsible for primary control and corrective action.
    2. provide no surprises.
    3. provide data on worker performance to supervision for punitive action.
    4. contribute to a reduction in quality cost.
    5. none of the above.

10. The mean of either a discrete or a continuous distribution can always be visualized as:
    1. the point where 50% of the values are to the left side and 50% are to the right side.
    2. it's center of gravity.
    3. the point where the most values in the distribution occur.
    4. all of the above.

11. Parts in use during the "wearout" portion of the part life cycle curve will exhibit:
   1. a constant failure rate.
   2. a decreasing failure rate.
   3. a low failure rate.
   4. an increasing failure rate.

12. When introducing a new product to the manufacturing phase of the product's life, the most important justification for a process capability study--after a pilot run for stability, but during a controlled preproduction operation is:
   1. it will prove design feasibility.
   2. it will establish machine capability.
   3. it will provide manufacturing engineering with the basis for a preventive maintenance schedule.
   4. it will determine the degree of conformance of the tools, materials, and operators with design specifications and economic yield requirements.

13. Which of the following elements is least necessary to a good corrective action feedback report:
   1. what caused the failure.
   2. who caused the failure.
   3. what correction has been made.
   4. when the correction is effective.

14. When analyzing quality cost data during the initial stages of management's emphasis on quality control and corrective action as part of a product improvement program, one normally expects to see:
   1. increased prevention costs and decreased appraisal costs.
   2. decreased internal failure costs.
   3. increased appraisal costs with little change in prevention costs.
   4. increased external failure costs.
   5. none of the above.

15. The inspection plan for a new product line may include:
   1. detailed production schedule.
   2. sampling procedures and techniques.
   3. internal techniques for control and segregation of conforming or nonconforming product.
   4. answers 1 and 2 above.
   5. answers 1,2, and 3 above.

16. Which is not a limit gage?
   1. ring gage
   2. radius gage
   3. vernier height gage
   4. gage blocks

17. Criteria for a comprehensive acceptance inspection system include which of the following?
   1. it should encourage and assist the supplier to improve the quality of his product.
   2. it should be easy to administer and economical in cost.
   3. it should enable the purchaser to accept all conforming items and to reject all nonconforming items.
   4. all of the above.

18. In nonparametric statistics:
   1. no assumptions are made concerning the distribution from which the samples are taken.
   2. the parameters of the distribution do not relate to the parameters of the sample.
   3. the sample and the distribution must have no parameters in common.
   4. none of the above.

19. Data from which of the following investigations would not normally be included in auditing a complete quality system:
   1. examination of all items produced.
   2. examination of customer needs and the adequacy of design specifications in reflecting these needs.
   3. examination of vendor product specifications and monitoring procedures.
   4. examination of customer quality complaints and adequacy for corrective action.

20. The terms "critical," "major", and "minor" or "incidental" may be used in planning for:
   1. classification of defects.
   2. classification of characteristics.
   3. acceptance sampling.
   4. all of the above.
   5. none of the above.

21. When we arrange a set of measurements in order of magnitude and indicate the frequency associated with each measurement, we have constructed:
   1. a grouped frequency distribution.
   2. a cumulative frequency distribution.
   3. an ungrouped frequency distribution.
   4. a bar graph.
   5. a histogram.

22. A qualification test is used to determine that design and selected production methods will yield a product that conforms to specification. An acceptance is used to determine that a completed product conforms to design. On this basis, a destructive test can be used for:
    1. qualification only.
    2. qualification or acceptance.
    3. acceptance only.
    4. neither qualification nor acceptance.

23. What four functions are necessary to have an acceptable calibration system covering measuring and test equipment in a written procedure?
    1. calibration sources, calibration intervals, environmental conditions, and sensitivity required for use.
    2. calibration sources, calibration intervals, humidity control and utilization of published standards.
    3. calibration sources, calibration intervals, environmental conditions under which equipment is calibrated, controls for unsuitable equipment.
    4. list of standards, identification report, certificate number and recall records.
    5. all of the above.

24. Outside endorsements or approvals, such as underwriter's laboratories fees, are usually considered which of the following quality costs:
    1. external failure.
    2. appraisal.
    3. prevention.
    4. internal failure.
    5. none of the above.

25. Why would inspection by variables be superior to inspection by attributes?
    1. inspection by variables is easier to administer than inspection by attributes.
    2. inspectors like inspection by variables better than inspection by attributes.
    3. more information is obtained when inspection by variables is utilized.
    4. inspection by variables is usually more economical than inspection by attributes.
    5. inspection by variables makes more sense than inspection by attributes.

26. What item(s) should be included by management when establishing a quality audit function within their organization?
    1. proper positioning of the audit function within their organization.
    2. a planned audit approach, efficient and timely audit reporting.
    3. selection of capable audit personnel.
    4. management objectivity toward the quality program audit concept.
    5. all of the above.

27. In control chart theory, the distribution of the number of defects per unit follows very closely the:
    1. normal distribution.
    2. binomial distribution.
    3. chi-square distribution.
    4. poisson distribution.

28. The "least squares method" is used in:
    1. the central limit theorem.
    2. calculating "sigma squared."
    3. calculating "sigma squared" from "s squared."
    4. calculating a best fit regression line.
    5. inspecting hole locations.

29. The expression $\frac{x!}{x!(x-n)!} p'^x (1-p')^{n-x}$ is the general term for:
    1. poisson distribution.
    2. pascal distribution.
    3. hypergeometric distribution.
    4. binomial distribution.
    5. none of the above.

30. Assurance bears the same relation to the quality function that _____ does to the accounting function.
    1. vacation
    2. audit
    3. variable overhead
    4. control

31. A null hypothesis requires several assumptions, a basic one of which is:
    1. that the variables are dependent.
    2. that the variables are independent.
    3. that the sample size is adequate.
    4. that the confidence interval is plus or minus 2 standard deviations.
    5. that the correlation coefficient is -0.95.

32. The appropriate mathematical model for describing the sampling distribution from a controlled process in which 'p-bar' = 0.05 is:
    1. the normal curve.
    2. the binomial distribution with p'=0.05.
    3. the binomial distribution with p'=0.95.
    4. the alpha level.

33. For a given number of degrees of freedom, as the variability among means (groups, columns) increases relative to the variability within groups:
    1. the f-ratio decreases.
    2. the f-ratio increases.
    3. the f-ratio is unaffected.
    4. the risk of a type I error increases.
    5. cannot answer without knowing the number of observations.

34. Your operation requires infrequent vendor shipments of a relatively small number of parts for a critical assembly. Desiring the best protection for the lowest cost, you advise the chief inspector that the most appropriate sampling plan for receiving inspection should be one developed from:
    1. the poisson distribution.
    2. the hypergeometric distribution.
    3. the binomial distribution.
    4. the log normal distribution.
    5. the gaussian (normal) distribution.

PART II: APPLICATIONS

1. One of the following is <u>not</u> a factor to consider in establishing quality information equipment cost:
   1. debugging cost
   2. amortization period
   3. design cost
   4. replacement parts and spares
   5. book cost

2. Failure mode, effect, and criticality analysis (fmeca)
   is primarily for the purpose of:
   1. learning as much about the item as possible after
      qualification test.
   2. determining the way an item will most likely fail to
      help obtain design and procedural safeguards against
      such failure.
   3. determining, by extensive analysis, the reliability
      of an item.
   4. determining the cause of a failure, by dissecting
      the item, to help obtain corrective action.

3. A vendor quality control plan has been adopted; which of
   the following would you advise top management to be <u>least</u>
   effective?
   1. product audits
   2. source inspection
   3. certificate of analysis
   4. certificate of compliance
   5. pre-award surveys

4. When planning a system for processing quality data or for
   keeping inspection and other quality records, the first
   step should be to:
   1. depict the system in a flow chart.
   2. hire a statistician.
   3. investigate applicable data processing equipment.
   4. determine the cost of operating the system.
   5. start coding the input data.

5. One method to control inspection costs even without a
   budget is by comparing _____ as a ratio to productive
   machine time to produce the product.
   1. product cost
   2. company profit
   3. inspection hours
   4. scrap material

6. If, in a designed experiment, you obtained an f-ratio of 0.68 with 2 and 20 degrees of freedom, you would conclude that:
   1. there were no significant differences among the means.
   2. you had made an error.
   3. the variances were equal.
   4. the null hypothesis was rejected.
   5. all of the above.

7. You have been assigned as a quality engineer to a small company. The quality control manager desires some cost data and the accounting department reported that the following information is available: production inspection, $14,185; test inspection, $4,264; procurement inspection, $2,198; shop labor, $141,698; shop rework, $1,402; first article, $675; engineering analysis (rework), $845; repair service (warrantees), $298; quality engineering, $2,175; design engineering salaries, $241,151; quality equipment, $18,745; training, $275; receiving laboratories, $385; underwriter's laboratories, $1,200; installation service cost, $9,000; scrap, $1,182; and calibration service, $794. What are the preventive costs?
   1. $3,727
   2. $23,701
   3. $23,026
   4. $3,295
   5. $2,450

8. A process is turning out end-items that have defects of type a or type b or both in them. If the probability of a type a defect is 0.10 and of a type b defect is 0.20, the probability that an end item will have no defects is:
   1. .02
   2. .28
   3. .30
   4. .72
   5. .68

9. Fixed gages:
   1. measure only one or more dimensions.
   2. measure only one dimension.
   3. are all made of tool steel.
   4. are a fast method of checking parts.

10. "Beauty defects" can best be described for inspection acceptance purposes by:
    1. simply stating that such defects are unacceptable.
    2. verbally describing rejection criteria.
    3. leaving them up to the inspector.
    4. establishing visual standards and/or samples describing the defects.
    5. establishing written standards describing the defects.

11. When using an inside or outside caliper, care must be taken to get the proper:
    1. slip.
    2. depth.
    3. grip.
    4. feel.

12. You have just returned from a two week vacation and are going over with your QC manager the control charts which have been maintained during your absence. He calls your attention to the fact that one of the x-bar charts shows the last 50 points to be very near the center line. What explanation would you offer him?
    1. Somebody "goofed" in the original calculation of the control limits.
    2. The process standard deviation has decreased during the time the last 50 samples were taken and nobody thought to recompute the control limits.
    3. This is a terrible situation. I'll get on it right away and see what the trouble is. I hope we haven't produced too much scrap.
    4. This is fine. The closer the points are to the center line the better our control.

13. The distinguishing feature of the optical comparator is that adjustments for measurement are observed on a:
    1. screen.
    2. reticle coordinator.
    3. dial indicator.
    4. rotating stage.

14. During the pre-award survey at a potential key supplier, you discover the existence of a quality control manual. This means:
    1. that a quality system has been developed.
    2. that a quality system has been implemented.
    3. that the firm is quality conscious.
    4. that the firm has a quality manager.
    5. all of the above.

15. You have been asked to appraise the new quality data
    system developed by your statistical services group; which
    of the following measures need <u>not</u> be considered during
    your evaluation of the effectiveness of that quality data
    system?
    1. The information is resulting in timely and effec-
       tive corrective action.
    2. The system is being adequately maintained.
    3. The reports are being distributed monthly.
    4. Paper work is being held to a minimum.

16. In analyzing the cost data below:

    $ 20,000 = final test
      350,000 = field warranty costs
      170,000 = reinspection and retest
       45,000 = loss or disposition of surplus stock
        4,000 = vendor quality surveys
       30,000 = rework

    We might conclude that:
    1. internal failure costs can be decreased.
    2. prevention cost is too low a proportion of the
       quality costs.
    3. appraisal costs should be increased.
    4. nothing can be concluded.

17. Select one single sampling plan from MIL-STD-105D that
    meets the following requirements: lot size=1000; AQL=
    0.65%; inspection level II; tightened inspection:
    1. sample size=125; ac=1;re=2
    2. sample size=200; ac=1;re=2
    3. sample size= 80; ac=1;re=2
    4. sample size= 50; ac=0;re=2
    5. sample size= 80; ac=8;re=9

18. Quality cost analysis has shown that appraisal costs are
    apparently too high in relation to sales. Which of the
    following actions probably would <u>not</u> be considered in
    pursing this problem?
    1. work sampling in inspection and test areas.
    2. adding inspectors to reduce scrap.
    3. pareto analysis of quality costs.
    4. considering elimination of some test operation.
    5. comparing appraisal costs to bases other than sales--
       for example, direct labor, value added, etc.

19. An inspection plan is set up to randomly sample 3' of a 100' cable and accept the cable if no flaws are found in the 3' length. What is the probability that a cable with an average of 1 flaw per foot will be rejected by the plan?
    1. .05
    2. .95
    3. .72
    4. .03
    5. .10

20. The primary responsibility for follow-up on corrective action commitments after an audit report usually rests with:
    1. production management.
    2. quality engineering.
    3. the function being audited.
    4. the audit group.

21. Which of the following techniques would not be used in a quality audit?
    1. select samples only from completed lots.
    2. examine samples from the viewpoint of a critical customer.
    3. audit only those items that have produced customer complaints.
    4. use audit information in future design planning.
    5. frequency of audit to depend on economic and quality requirements.

22. The most important step in vendor certification is to:
    1. obtain copies of the vendor's handbook.
    2. familiarize vendor with quality requirements.
    3. analyze vendor's first shipment.
    4. visit the vendor's plant.

23. During the design review stage for new equipment you recommend that a human factors use test be performed under one of the following conditions:
    1. on a production model if possible.
    2. not combined with engineering tests on the same equipment.
    3. it demonstrates the ability of personnel to perform the required functions using the equipment.
    4. all of the above.

24. A lot of 50 pieces contains 5 defectives. A sample of 2 is drawn without replacement. The probability that both will be defective is:
    1. .4000
    2. .0100
    3. .0010
    4. .0082
    5. .0093

25. Suppose that 5 bad electron tubes get mixed up with 8 good tubes. If 2 tubes are drawn simultaneously, what is the probability that both are good?
    1. 8/13
    2. 14/39
    4. 7/13
    5. 36/91

26. Maintainability of an equipment may be measured in terms of:
    1. maintenance manhours.
    2. repair time.
    3. maintenance dollar cost.
    4. all of the above.

27. Gages that tell how much a dimension varies from a specification are called:
    1. accurators.
    2. depth gages.
    3. indicating gages.
    4. tolerators.

28. You have just conducted a designed experiment at three levels a,b, and c yielding the following "coded" data:

a	b	c
6	5	3
3	9	4
5	1	2
2		

    As a major step in your analysis you calculate the degrees of freedom for the "error" sum of squares to be:
    1. 7
    2. 9
    3. 3
    4. 2
    5. 10

29. A random sample of 10 items was taken from lot a, 20 from
    lot b, and 30 from lot c. The three lots contained the
    same type of material. Each of the samples yielded the
    same mean. Which of the following statements is true
    concerning the standard deviation of the samples?
    1. The standard deviation of lot c is the largest.
    2. The standard deviation of lot a is the largest.
    3. The standard deviation of lot c is three times as
       large as that of the lot a sample.
    4. None of the above statements can be made.

30. The modern approach to quality cost is to:
    1. concentrate on external failures; they are impor-
       tant to the business since they represent customer
       acceptance.
    2. consider the four cost segments and their general
       trends.
    3. budget each cost element such as amounts for inspec-
       tion, quality control salaries, scrap, etc.
    4. reduce expenditures on each segment individually.
    5. make annual budget cuts where cost elements show
       major variances.

31. The percentages of quality costs are distributed as
    follows:

    preventive   12%
    appraisal   28%
    internal failure   40%

    We conclude:
    1. we should invest more money in prevention.
    2. expenditures for failures are excessive.
    3. the amount spent for appraisal seems about right.
    4. nothing.

32. One of the major hazards in the material review board
    procedure is the tendency of the board to emphasize only
    the disposition function and to neglect the _____
    _____ function.
    1. statistical analysis
    2. corrective action
    3. material evaluation
    4. tolerance review
    5. manufacturing methods

33. One of the most important techniques in making a training program effective is to:
    1. concentrate only on developing knowledge and skills needed to do a good job.
    2. transmit all of the information that is even remotely related to the function.
    3. set individual goals instead of group goals.
    4. give people meaningful measures of performance.

34. You have just been put in charge of incoming inspection and have decided to institute a sampling plan on a small gear which your company uses in considerable quantity. The vendor ships them in lots of 1000. You have decided to use MIL-STD-105D, inspection level II, and an AQL = 4.0 percent. Naturally, your inspectors, never having used scientific sampling, are interested in seeing how it works. The first lot is inspected and accepted. One of the inspectors says: "This means that the lot is not more than four percent defective." Assuming that the sample was randomly taken and no inspection errors were made, which one of the following would you accept?
    1. The inspector's statement is correct.
    2. The probability of accepting is about 0.99.
    3. You should go to reduced sampling.
    4. The lot may be ten percent defective.
    5. All of the above are correct.

ANSWERS TO FINAL EXAM

PART I: PRINCIPLES		PART II: APPLICATIONS	
Question	Answer	Question	Answer
1	4	1	5
2	3	2	2
3	2	3	4
4	4	4	1
5	4	5	3
6	3	6	1
7	2	7	5
8	4	8	4
9	3	9	4
10	2	10	4
11	4	11	4
12	4	12	2
13	2	13	1
14	3	14	1
15	5	15	3
16	3	16	2
17	4	17	1
18	1	18	2
19	1	19	2
20	4	20	4
21	3	21	3
22	2	22	2
23	3	23	3
24	2	24	4
25	3	25	2
26	5	26	4
27	4	27	3
28	4	28	1
29	5	29	4
30	2	30	2
31	2	31	4
32	2	32	2
33	2	33	4
34	2	34	4

ASQC Quality Engineer Certification Examination

Introduction by
David C. Leaman
Education Director

On June 15, 1968, after a six month "grandfather" period, the first written examinations were conducted for qualified candidates wishing to become ASQC-Certified Quality Engineers (CQE). Then 149 became certified, including four Canadians, taking the examination in 15 locations. In contrast, last June, 658 candidates were scheduled in 102 locations in four countries!

This CQE program (followed later by a second professional level program for reliability engineers and a paraprofessional certification for quality technicians) became "the cutting edge of the Society," as termed by one of its founders, Professor John Henry (emeritus of the University of Illinois). ASQC pioneered a concept of technical specialty certification now practiced by 13 technical societies and numerous other professional organizations. Certification has done more to promote the quality profession and enhance the Society's image than any other ASQC program.

Acceptance by industry and government has been beyond our utmost expectations. Indeed, a leading placement firm reports that about 50 percent of all requests for quality personnel specify ASQC certification.

Much of this success is due to a solid foundation laid by many ASQC members with vision and determination, including Dr. Max Astrachan, who administered the difficult "grandfather" period, and Hy Pitt who administered the first examinations.

As a study aid, one of the early examinations was reprinted in the October 1972 *Quality Progress* — "certification issue," together with a developmental history of the program. This became so popular, that the ASQC Certification Committee established the policy of publishing previously given examinations (from the various programs) as study aids every two years. Thus, another CQE examination appeared in October '74 *QP* followed by a reprinted Certified Reliability Engineer (CRE) examination in February '76. In this issue we publish a third CQE examination, and present an updated bibliography plus the names of those most recently certified through the program. Note that the evolving QE body of knowledge includes the expanded areas of product liability and product safety.

As added inducement to proper study, the correct answers are listed separately after the bibliography section. NOTE: there is no guarantee that any of these questions will appear as shown on future examinations; rather, this is offered as "typical" for instructional purposes. It is hoped that this will be of special value to people remote from Section-sponsored exam preparation courses. Aided by an extensive computerized analysis, recent examinations have been well within our 95/20 target; i.e. questions answered correctly by 95 percent or more of the candidates are too easy or nondiscriminating, while those answered by 20 percent or fewer are too difficult or ambiguous. In all cases, the biserial and point biserial correlations should be positive and of a discriminating level.

As administrative requirements are met, we will publish other examinations from all three programs.

PRINCIPLES

1. A p-chart is a type of control chart for:
   1. plotting bar-stock lengths from receiving inspection samples
   2. plotting fraction defective results from shipping inspection samples
   3. plotting defects per unit from in-process inspection samples
   4. answers 1, 2, and 3 above
   5. answers 1 and 3 only

2. The sensitivity of a p-chart to changes in quality is:
   1. equal to that of a range chart
   2. equal to that of a chart for averages
   3. equal to that of a c-chart
   4. equal to that of a u-chart
   5. none of the above

3. A p-chart has exhibited statistical control over a period of time. However, the average fraction defective is too high to be satisfactory. Improvement can be obtained by:
   1. a change in the basic design of the product
   2. instituting 100% inspection
   3. a change in the production process through substitution of new tooling or machinery
   4. all of the above answers are correct except number 2
   5. all of the above answers are correct except number 3

4. Consumer's risk is defined as:
   1. Accepting an unsatisfactory lot as satisfactory.
   2. Passing a satisfactory lot as satisfactory.
   3. An alpha risk.
   4. A 5% risk of accepting an unsatisfactory lot.

5. In MIL-STD-105D, the AQL is always determined at what P on the OC-curve?
   1. 0.05
   2. 0.10
   3. 0.90
   4. 0.95
   5. none of the above

6. If a distribution is skewed to the left, the median will always be:
   1. less than the mean
   2. between the mean and the mode
   3. greater than the mode
   4. equal to the mean
   5. equal to the mode

7. The steeper the OC-curve, the:
   1. less protection for both producer and consumer
   2. more protection for both producer and consumer
   3. the lower the AQL
   4. the smaller the sample size

8. The sum of the squared deviations of a group of measurements from their mean divided by the number of measurements equals:
   1. σ
   2. σ^2
   3. zero
   4. X
   5. the mean deviation

9. In determining a process average fraction defective using inductive or inferential statistics, we use _____ computed from _____ to make inferences about _____.
   1. statistics, samples, populations
   2. populations, samples, populations
   3. samples, statistics, populations
   4. samples, populations, samples
   5. statistics, populations, statistics

10. Which of the following statistical measures of variability is *not* dependent on the exact value of every measurement?
    1. interquartile range
    2. variance
    3. range
    4. coefficient of variation
    5. none of the above

11. When used together for variables data, which of the following is the most useful pair of quantities in Quality Control?
    1. $\overline{X}$, R
    2. $\overline{X}$, η
    3. R, σ
    4. $\overline{p}$, η
    5. AQL, p′

12. For an operaion requiring shipments from your vendor of small lots of fixed size, the sampling plan used for receiving inspection should have its OC curve developed using:
    1. the Poisson distribution
    2. the Hypergeometric distribution
    3. the Binomial distribution
    4. the Log Normal distribution
    5. the Gaussian (normal) distribution

13. Two quantities which uniquely determine a single sampling attributes plan are:
    1. AOQL and LTPD
    2. sample size and rejection number
    3. AQL and producer's risk
    4. LTPD and consumer's risk
    5. AQL and LTPD

14. Selection of a sampling plan from the Dodge-Romig AOQL sampling tables:
    1. requires an estimate of the AOQ
    2. requires an estimate of the process average
    3. requires sorting of rejected lots
    4. requires larger samples than MIL-STD-105D for equivalent quality assurance
    5. requires that we assume a consumer's risk of .05

15. The expression $\dfrac{v^X \cdot e^{-\mu}}{x!}$ is the general term for the:
    1. Hypergeometric distribution
    2. Pascal distribution
    3. Poisson distribution
    4. Binomial distribution
    5. none of the above

16. If, in a t-test, alpha is .01:
    1. 1% of the time we will say that there is a real difference, when there really is not a difference
    2. 1% of the time we will make a correct inference
    3. 1% of the time we will say that there is no real difference, but in reality there is a difference
    4. 99% of the time we will make an incorrect inference
    5. 99% of the time the null hypothesis will be correct

17. Suppose that, given X = 50, and Z = ± 1.96, we established 95% confidence limits for μ of 30 and 70. This means that:
    1. the probability that μ = 50 is .05
    2. the probability that μ = 50 is .95
    3. the probability that the interval contains μ is .05
    4. the probability that the interval contains μ is .95
    5. none of the above

18. MIL-STD-105D sampling plans allow reduced inspection when four requirements are met. One of these is:
    1. inspection level I is specified

2. 10 lots have been on normal inspection and none have been rejected
3. the process average is less than the AOQL
4. the maximum percent defective is less than the AQL
5. all of the above

19. The AQL for a given sampling plan is 1.0%. This means that:
    1. the producer takes a small risk of rejecting product which is 1.0% defective or better
    2. all accepted lots are 1.0% defective or better
    3. the average quality limit of the plan is 1.0%
    4. the average quality level of the plan is 1.0%
    5. all lots are 1.0% defective or better

20. If X and Y are distributed normally and independently, the variance of X-Y is equal to:
    1. $\sigma_x^2 \; 2 \; \sigma_y^2$
    2. $\sigma_x - \sigma_y^2$
    3. $\sqrt{\sigma_x^2 + \sigma^{y2}}$
    4. $\sqrt{\sigma_y^2 - \sigma_y^2}$

21. The mean of either a discrete or a continuous distribution can always be visualized as:
    1. the point where 50% of the values are to the left side and 50% are to the right side
    2. its center of gravity
    3. the point where the most values in the distribution occur
    4. all of the above

22. In control chart theory, the distribution of the number of defects per unit follows very closely the:
    1. normal distribution
    2. binomial distribution
    3. Chi-square distribution
    4. Poisson distribution

23. A Latin Square design is noted for its straightforward analysis of interaction effects. The above statement is:
    1. true in every case
    2. true sometimes; depending on the size of the square
    3. true only for Greco-Latin Squares
    4. false in every case
    5. false except for Greco-Latin Squares

24. Considerations to be made prior to the use of any sampling plan is (are):
    1. the consumer's and producer's risks must be specified
    2. the method of selecting samples must be specified
    3. the characteristics to be inspected must be specified
    4. the conditions must be specified (material accumulated in lots or inspected by continuous sampling)
    5. all of the above

25. The probability of accepting material produced at an acceptable quality level is defined as:
    1. α
    2. β
    3. AQL
    4. $1 - \alpha$
    5. $1 - \beta$

26. A null hypothesis requires several assumptions, a basic one of which is:
    1. that the variables are dependent
    2. that the variables are independent
    3. that the sample size is adequate
    4. that the confidence interval is ± 2 standard deviation
    5. that the correlation coefficient is -0.95.

27. One use for a Student t-test is to determine whether or not differences exist in:
    1. variability
    2. quality costs
    3. correlation coefficients
    4. averages
    5. none of these

28. The "Least Squares Method" is used in:
    1. the Central Limit Theorem
    2. calculating σ^2
    3. calculating σ^2 from σ^2
    4. calculating a best fit regression line
    5. inspecting hole locations

29. AOQL means:
    1. average outgoing quality level
    2. average outgoing quality limit

3. average outside quality limit
4. anticipated optimum quality level

30. In nonparametric statistics:
1. no assumptions are made concerning the distribution from which the samples are taken
2. the parameters of the distribution do not relate to the parameters of the sample
3. the sample and the distribution must have no parameters in common
4. none of the above

31. Given 6 books how many sets can be arranged in lots of 3 but always in a different order?
1. 18 sets
2. 54 sets
3. 108 sets
4. 120 sets

32. The probability of observing at least one defective in a random sample of size ten drawn from a population that has been producing, on the average, ten percent defective units is:
1. $(0.10)^{10}$
2. $(0.90)^{10}$
3. $1 - (0.10)^{10}$
4. $1 - (0.90)^{10}$
5. $(0.10)(0.90)^9$

33. In preparing a Quality Policy concerning a product line for your company you should *not*:
1. specify the means by which quality performance is measured
2. develop criteria for identifying risk situations, and specify whose approval is required when there are known risks
3. load the policy with procedural matters or ordinary functional responsibilities
4. identify responsibilities for dispositioning defective hardware
5. answers 2 and 4 above

34. A fully developed position description for a Quality Engineer must contain clarification of:
1. responsibility
2. accountability
3. authority
4. answers 1 and 3 above
5. answers 1, 2, and 3 above

35. "Good Housekeeping" is an important quality factor in a supplier's plant because:
1. it promotes good working conditions
2. it minimizes fire hazards
3. it enhances safer operations
4. it reflects favorably on the efficiency and management of a company
5. all of the above

36. The purpose of a Quality Manual is to:
1. use it as a basis for every Quality decision.
2. standardize the methods and decisions of a department
3. optimize company performance in addition to improving the effectiveness of the Quality department
4. make it possible to handle every situation in exactly the same manner

37. Essential to the success of any Quality Control organization is the receipt of:
1. adequate and stable resources
2. clear and concise project statements
3. delegation of authority to accomplish the objective
4. all of the above

38. The inspection plan for a new product line may include:
1. detailed production schedule
2. sampling procedures and techniques
3. internal techniques for control and segregation of conforming or nonconforming product
4. answers 1 and 2 above
5. answers 1, 2, and 3 above

39. Classification of defects is most essential as a prior step to a valid establishment of:
1. design characteristics to be inspected
2. vendor specifications of critical parts
3. process control points
4. economical sampling inspection
5. a product audit check list

40. The first step, and most important in establishing a good corporate quality plan is:

1. determining customer requirements
2. determining manufacturing process capabilities
3. evaluating vendor quality system
4. ensuring quality participation in design review

41. If not specifically required by the product drawing(s) or specification, non-destructive test (NDT) may be required during production and/or during acceptance at the discretion of the quality engineer responsible for the inspection planning. This statement is:
1. false — because testing is limited to that specified by the design engineer
2. true — because NDT is a form of inspection (with enhanced senses) not a functional test
3. false — the QE may impose NDT as he believes necessary but cannot delete it without design engineering permission
4. true — because all acceptance testing and inspection requirements are up to quality engineering

42. When giving instructions to those who will perform a task, the communication process is completed:
1. when the worker goes to his work station to do the task
2. when the person giving the instruction has finished talking
3. when the worker acknowledges these instructions by describing how he will perform the task
4. when the worker says that he understands the instructions

43. Some product specifications contain a section called "Quality Assurance" which contains the design engineer's requirements for acceptance testing. The relationship between the acceptance test procedure for a product and the acceptance test portion of the quality assurance section of the specification for that product is:
1. test procedure must require testing for the characteristics listed in the acceptance test portion of the specification and the quality engineer can add additional tests he believes necessary
2. test procedure must require testing for characteristics selected from the acceptance test portion of the specification but does not have to require testing for all such characteristics
3. test procedure must require testing for those and only those characteristics listed in the acceptance test portion of the specification
4. the acceptance test portion of the specification is a good general guide to the test procedure writer and the test procedure reviewer but is not mandatory in any way

44. The primary reason that nonconforming material should be identified and segregated is:
1. so that the cause of nonconformity can be determined
2. to provide statistical information for the "zero defects" program
3. so it cannot be used in production without proper authorization
4. to obtain samples of poor workmanship for use in the company's training program
5. so that responsibility can be determined and disciplinary action taken

45. A quality program has the best foundation for success when it is initiated by:
1. a certified quality engineer
2. contractual requirements
3. chief executive of company
4. production management
5. an experienced quality manager

46. A quality manual:
1. is a static document, best used for Public Relations purposes
2. is a benchmark against which current practice may be audited
3. is the responsibility of all company departments
4. should be approved only by the quality department
5. is not needed in most organizations

47. When specifying the "10:1 calibration principle," we are referring to what?
1. the ratio of operators to inspectors
2. the ratio of quality engineers to metrology personnel
3. the ratio of main scale to vernier scale calibration
4. the ratio of calibration standard accuracy to calibrated instrument accuracy
5. none of the above

48. A qualification test is used to determine that design and selected production methods will yield a product that conforms to specification. An acceptance test is used to determine that a completed product conforms to design. On this basis, a destructive test can be used for:
1. qualification only
2. qualification or acceptance

3. acceptance only
4. neither qualification nor acceptance

49. In geometric dimensioning and tolerancing the symbol M means:
    1. maximum material condition
    2. use a micrometer to check
    3. machined surface
    4. measure at this point

50. Which is not a limit gage?
    1. ring gage
    2. radius gage
    3. vernier height gage
    4. gage blocks

51. Sensory testing is used in a number of industries to evaluate their products. Which of the following is not a sensory test?
    1. ferritic annial test
    2. triangle test
    3. duo-trio test
    4. ranking test
    5. paired-comparison test

52. X-rays and gamma rays are both commonly used in industrial radiography for detecting flaws in materials. Which of the following statements most correctly describes the differences between these two types of radiation?
    1. X-rays ave wave lengths 10^{-8} to 10^{-10} cm, whereas gamma rays have wave lengths 10^{-9} to 10^{-12} cm.
    2. Both originate from the nucleus of an atom.
    3. X-rays are lower energy than gamma rays.
    4. They are similar, both being electromagnetic radiation,m however, differing in origin.

53. Criteria for a comprehensive acceptance inspection system include which of the following?
    1. It should encourage and assist the supplier to improve the quality of his product.
    2. It should be easy to administer and economical in cost.
    3. It should enable the purchaser to accept all conforming items and to reject all nonconforming items.
    4. All of the above.

54. The major purpose of test and inspection is to:
    1. remove all defects to prevent shipment of sub-standard product
    2. find which operations are problems
    3. identify poor operators
    4. develop information to enable corrective action
    5. keep costs down by finding defects early in the cycle

55. Measuring and test equipment are calibrated to:
    1. comply with federal regulations
    2. assure their precision
    3. determine and/or assure their accuracy
    4. check the validity of reference standards
    5. accomplish all of the above

56. Why would inspection by variables be superior to inspection by attributes?
    1. Inspection by variables is easier to administer than inspection by attributes.
    2. Inspectors like inspection by variables better than inspection by attributes.
    3. More information is obtained when inspection by variables is utilized.
    4. Inspection by variables is usually more economical than inspection by attributes.
    5. Inspection by variables makes more sense than inspection by attributes.

57. A basic requirement of most gage calibration system specifications is:
    1. all inspection equipment must be calibrated with master gage blocks
    2. gages must be color coded for identification
    3. equipment shall be labeled or coded to indicate date calibrated, by whom, and date due for next calibration
    4. gages must be identified with a tool number
    5. all of the above

58. What four functions are necessary to have an acceptable calibration system covering measuring and test equipment in a written procedure?
    1. calibration sources, calibration intervals, environmental conditions, and sensitivity required for use
    2. calibration sources, calibration intervals, humidity control and utilization of published standards

3. calibration sources, calibration intervals, environmental conditions under which equipment is calibrated, controls for unsuitable equipment
4. list of standards, identification report, certificate number and recall records
5. all of the above

59. A variable measurement of a dimension should include:
    1. an estimate of the accuracy of the measurement process
    2. a controlled measurement procedure
    3. a numerical value for the parameter being measured
    4. an estimate of the precision of the measurement process
    5. all of the above

60. When looking for existing sources of internal failure cost data, which of the following is usually the best source available?
    1. operating budgets
    2. salesmen's field reports
    3. labor and material cost documents
    4. returned material reports
    5. purchase orders

61. Of the following, which are typically appraisal costs?
    1. vendor surveys and vendor faults
    2. quality planning and quality reports
    3. drawing control centers and material dispositions
    4. quality audits and final inspection
    5. none of the above

62. Which of the following cost elements is normally a prevention cost?
    1. receiving inspection
    2. outside endorsements or approvals
    3. design of quality measurement equipment
    4. all of the above

63. When analyzing quality cost data gathered during the *initial* stages of a new management emphasis on quality control and corrective action as part of a product improvement program, one normally expects to see:
    1. increased prevention costs and decreased appraisal costs
    2. increased appraisal costs with little change in prevention costs
    3. decreased internal failure costs
    4. decreased total quality costs
    5. all of these

64. Quality costs are best classified as:
    1. cost of inspection and test, cost of quality engineering, cost of quality administration and cost of quality equipment
    2. direct, indirect and overhead
    3. cost of prevention, cost of appraisal and cost of failure
    4. unnecessary
    5. none of the above

65. Which of the following bases of performance measurement (denominators), when related to operating quality costs (numerator), would provide reliable indicator(s) to quality management for overall evaluation of the effectiveness of the company's quality program? Quality costs per:
    1. total manufacturing costs
    2. unit produced
    3. total direct labor dollars
    4. only one of the above
    5. any two of the above

66. Quality cost data:
    1. must be maintained when the end product is for the government
    2. must be mailed to the contracting officer on request
    3. is often an effective means of identifying quality problem areas
    4. all of the above

67. Operating quality costs can be related to different volume bases. An example of volume base that could be used would be:
    1. direct labor cost
    2. standard manufacturing cost
    3. processing cost
    4. sales
    5. all of the above

68. When operating a quality cost system, excessive costs can be identified when:
    1. appraisal costs exceed failure costs
    2. total quality costs exceed 10% of sales
    3. appraisal and failure costs are equal
    4. total quality costs exceed 4% of manufacturing costs
    5. there is no fixed rule-management experience must be used

69. Quality cost systems provide for defect prevention. Which of the following elements is primary to defect prevention?

1. corrective action
2. data collection
3. cost analysis
4. training

70. Which of the following is not a legitimate audit function?
   1. identify function reponsible for primary control and corrective action
   2. provide no surprises
   3. provide data on worker performance to supervision for punitive action
   4. contribute to a reduction in quality cost
   5. none of the above

71. In many programs, what is generally the weakest link in the quality auditing program?
   1. lack of adequate audit check lists
   2. scheduling of audits (frequency)
   3. audit reporting
   4. follow-up of corrective action implementation

72. What item(s) should be included by management when establishing a quality audit function within their organization?
   1. proper positioning of the audit function within the quality organization
   2. a planned audit approach, efficient and timely audit reporting and a method for obtaining effective corrective action
   3. selection of capable audit personnel
   4. management objectivity toward the quality program audit concept
   5. all of the above

73. Assurance bears the same relation to the quality function that _____ does to the accounting function.
   1. vacation
   2. audit
   3. variable overhead
   4. control

74. A pre-award survey of a potential supplier is best described as a _____ audit.
   1. compliance
   2. assessment
   3. quantitative
   4. all of these
   5. none of these

75. Which of the following best describes the "specific activity" type of audit?
   1. customer oriented sampling of finished goods
   2. evaluation for contractual compliance of quality system
   3. assessment or survey of potential vendor
   4. an inspection performance audit
   5. none of the above

76. Maintainability is:
   1. the probability of a system being restored to functional operation within a given period of time
   2. performing adequate maintenance on a system
   3. probability of survival of a system for a given period of time
   4. maintaining a machine in satisfactory working condition
   5. none of the above

77. In some reliability models redundancy may take the form of stand-by elements. What is the major disadvantage of such a model as regards its reliability?
   1. more costly
   2. reliability may be reduced by failure of sensing devices
   3. failure rates are generally high
   4. the system is too complex
   5. none of these

78. Product reliability is the probability of a product performing its intended function and under the operating conditions encountered. A significant element in this concept includes:
   1. probability
   2. performance
   3. time
   4. environment
   5. all of the above

Parts in use during the "wearout" portion of the part life cycle curve will exhibit:
   1. a constant failure rate
   2. a decreasing failure rate
   3. a low failure rate
   4. an increasing failure rate

80. Reliability, maintainability, and product safety improvements are most often economically accomplished during the _____ phase of a program.
   1. design and development
   2. prototype test
   3. production
   4. field operation
   5. redesign and retrofit

81. Quality information equipment:
   1. is used only by the Quality Control function
   2. is used only for the purpose of accepting or rejecting product
   3. makes measurements of either products or processes and feeds the resulting data back for decision making
   4. includes automatic electronic instruments but not go/no-go gages

82. In today's world, quality information documentation is called:
   1. end-item narrative
   2. hardware
   3. data pack
   4. software
   5. warrantee

83. The quality needs for historical information in the areas of specifications, performance reporting, complaint analysis, or run records would fall into which of the following computer applicatio categories?
   1. data accumulation
   2. data reduction analysis and reporting
   3. real-time process control
   4. statistical analysis
   5. information retrieval

84. In establishing a quality reporting and information feedback system primary consideration must be given to:
   1. number of inspection stations
   2. management approval
   3. timely feedback and corrective action
   4. historical preservation of data
   5. routing copy list

85. All quality information reports should be audited periodically to:
   1. determine their continued validity
   2. reappraise the routing or copy list
   3. determine their current effectiveness
   4. all of the above
   5. none of the above

86. McGregor's theory X manager is typified as one who operates from the following basic assumption about people working for him (select the one best answer):
   1. Performance can be improved through tolerance and trust.
   2. People have a basic need to produce.
   3. Status is more important than money.
   4. Self-actualization is the highest order of human need.
   5. People are lazy and are motivated by reward and punishment.

87. When installing a new system for collecting failure data in a manufacturing plant, the following approach is recommended:
   1. Issue a procedure written by a quality engineer without help from other departments to prevent a biased input from production test technicians.
   2. Have production write their own procedure.
   3. Use a procedure from another company.
   4. Enlist the collaboration of all affected departments in drafting and approving the procedure.
   5. None of the above.

88. Having designed a test fixture to performance requirements, the design should be carefully evaluated by the quality engineer to insure that it has included:
   1. low cost components
   2. printout capability
   3. human motor coordination factors
   4. mass production methods
   5. computer inputs

89. Quality motivation in industry should be directed at:
   1. manufacturing management
   2. procurement and engineering
   3. the quality assurance staff
   4. the working force
   5. all the above

90. In order to instill the quality control employee with the desire to perform to his utmost and optimum ability, which of the following

recognition for sustaining motivation has been found effective for most people?
1. recognition by issuance of monetary award
2. verbal recognition publicly
3. private verbal recognition
4. public recognition, plus non-monetary award
5. no recogntion; salary he obtains is sufficient motivation

APPLICATIONS

1. Determine the coefficient of variation for the last 500 pilot plant test runs of high temperature film having a mean of 900° Kelvin with a standard deviation of 54°:
   1. 6%
   2. 16.7%
   3. 0.06%
   4. 31%
   5. the reciprocal of the relative standard deviation

2. You determine that it is sometimes economical to permit X to go out of control when:
   1. the individual R's exceed R
   2. the cost of inspection is high
   3. 6σ is appreciably less than the difference between specification limits
   4. the $\overline{X}$ control limits are inside the drawing tolerance limits
   5. never

3. An electronics firm was experiencing high rejections in their multiple connector manufacturing departments. "P" Charts were introduced as part of a program to reduce defectives. Control limits were based on prior history, using the formula:

$$P' \pm 3 \sqrt{\frac{P'(100-P')}{N}}$$

Where P' is the historical value of percent defective and N is the number of pieces inspected each week. After six weeks the following record was accumulated:

Percent Defective

Dept.	P'	Week 1	Week 2	Week 3	Week 4	Week 5	Week 6
101	12	11	11	14	15	10	12
102	17	20	17	21	21	20	13
103	22	18	26	27	17	20	19
104	9	8	11	6	13	12	10
105	16	13	19	20	12	15	17
106	15	18	19	16	11	13	16

600 pieces were inspected each week in each department. Which department(s) exhibited a point or points out of control during the period?
   1. dept. 101
   2. dept. 102
   3. dept. 103
   4. dept. 104
   5. dept. 105

4. MIL-STD-105D is to be used to select a single sampling plan for lots of 8,000 under normal inspection, Level II, and an AQL of 2.5%. The exact AOQL for the plan is:
   1. 2.50%
   2. 3.00%
   3. 3.22%
   4. 3.30%
   5. 2.60%

5. A lot of 50 pieces contains 5 defectives. A sample of two is drawn without replacement. The probability that both will be defective is approximately:
   1. .4000
   2. .0100
   3. .0010
   4. .0082
   5. .0093

6. Large panes of plate glass contain on the average 0.25 flaws per pane. The standard deviation of the distribution of flaws is:
   1. .25
   2. .05
   3. .50
   4. .75
   5. none of the above

7. You have just returned from a two-week vaction and are going over with your QC manager, the control charts which have been maintained during your absence. He calls your attention to the fact that one of the X-charts shows the last 50 points to be very near the center line. In fact, they all seem to be within about one sigma of the center line. What explanation would you offer him?
   1. Somebody "goofed" in the original calculation of the control limits.
   2. The process standard deviation has decreased during the time the last 50 samples were taken and nobody thought to recompute the control limits.
   3. This is a terrible situation. I'll get on it right away and see what the trouble is. I hope we haven't produced too much scrap.
   4. This is fine. The closer the points are to the center line the better our control.

8. Your Quality Control Manager has asked you to make a study of the costs of using variables sampling as against attribute sampling for a pipe fitting. After searching the literature you find that the following sampling plans will give equal protection over the range of quality levels in which you are interested:

Type of Plan	Sample Size	Acceptance Criterion
Attributes	450	Ac = 10, Re = 11
Variables, sigma unknown	100	k = 2.0
Variables, sigma known	33	k = 2.0

Upon investigating the possible costs involved in each type of sampling with your accounting, production, and inspection departments, you arrive at the following figures:

	Attributes	Sigma Unknown	Sigma Known
Unit Sampling Cost	$ .05	.05	.05
Unit Inspection Cost	.05	.35	.3⁵
Unit Computation Cost	.00	.02	.
Lot Overhead Cost	6.00	18.00	40.00

Based on the above information, which sampling plan would you advise your inspector to use?
   1. Since they all give equal protection, it doesn't make any difference.
   2. Use attributes sampling.
   3. Use continuous sampling.
   4. Use variable sampling, sigma unknown.
   5. Use variable sampling, sigma known.

9. Suppose that 5 bad electron tubes get mixed up with 8 good tubes. If 2 tubes are drawn simultaneously, what is the probability that both are good?
   1. 8/13
   2. 14/39
   3. 7/12
   4. 7/13
   5. 36/91

10. The lengths of a certain bushing are normally distributed with mean $\overline{X}'$. How many standard deviation units, symmetrical about $\overline{X}'$, will include 80% of the lengths?
   1. ± 1.04
   2. ± 0.52
   3. ± 1.28
   4. ± 0.84

11. Three trainees were given the same lot of 50 pieces and asked to classify them as defective or non-defective, with the following results:

	Trainee 1	Trainee 2	Trainee 3	Total
Defective	17	30	25	72
Non-Defective	33	20	25	7⁸
Total	50	50	50	15ʋ

In determining whether or not there is a difference in the ability of the three trainees to properly classify the parts:
   1. the value of chi-square is about 6.90
   2. using a level of significance of 0.05, the critical value of chi-

square is 5.99

3. since the obtained chi-square is greater than 5.99, we reject the null hypothesis
4. all of the above
5. none of the above

12. A process is producing material which is 40% defective. Four pieces are selected at random for inspection. What is the probability of exactly one good piece being found in the sample?
    1. .870
    2. .575
    3. .346
    4. .130
    5. .154

13. An inspection plan is set up to randomly sample 3′ of a 100′ cable and accept the cable if no flaws are found in the 3′ length. What is the probability that a cable with an average of 1 flaw per foot will be rejected by the plan?
    1. .05
    2. .95
    3. .72
    4. .03
    5. .10

14. A process is turning out end-items which have defects of Type A or Type B or both in them. If the probability of a Type A defect is .10 and of a Type B defect is .20, the probability that an end item will have no defects is:
    1. .02
    2. .28
    3. .30
    4. .72
    5. .68

15. A bin contains 40 pills with a weight of 3.1 gm. each; 30 pills weighing 3.2 gms.; 10 pills weighing 3.3 gms. The weight of an average pill is found from:

    1. $\dfrac{3.1 + 3.2 + 3.3}{3}$ 3. $\dfrac{(3.1 + 3.2 + 3.3)(10 + 30 + 40)}{80}$

    2. $\dfrac{(3.1)(40) + 3.2(30) + 3.3(10)}{3}$ 4. $\dfrac{(3.1)(40) + 3.2(30) + 3.3(10)}{80}$

    If it was known that a population of 30,000 parts had a standard deviation of .05 seconds, what size sample would be required to maintain an error no greater than .01 seconds with a confidence level of 95%?
    1. 235
    2. 487
    3. 123
    4. 96
    5. 78

17. When you perform "one experiment" with "forthy-nine repetitions," what are the fifty experiments called?
    1. randomization
    2. replications
    3. planned grouping
    4. experimental pattern
    5. sequential

18. An $\overline{X}$ and R chart was prepared for an operation using twenty samples with five pieces in each sample. $\overline{X}$ was found to be 33.6 and R was 6.2. During production a sample of five was taken and the pieces measured 36, 43, 37, 34, and 38. At the time this sample was taken:
    1. both average and range were within control limits
    2. neither average nor range was within control limits
    3. only the average was outside control limits
    4. only the range was outside control limits
    5. the information given is not sufficient to construct an $\overline{X}$ and R chart using tables usually available.

19. You are to construct an OC curve. Which of the following cannot be used as an abscissa value?
    1. AOQL
    2. ASN
    3. AQL
    4. LTPD
    5. All of these can be abscissa values.

20. Determine whether the following two types of rockets have significantly different variances at the 5% level.

Rocket 1	Rocket 2
61 readings	31 readings
1,346.89 miles^2	2,237.29 miles^2

1. significant difference because Fcalc < F table
2. no significant difference because Fcalc < F table
3. significant difference because Fcalc > F table
4. no significant difference because Fcalc < F table

21. When small samples are used to estimate the standard deviation through use of the range statistic, sample subgroup sizes larger than 20 should not be used because:
    1. the number 20 causes calculation difficulties
    2. the efficiency of the range as an estimator of the standard deviation falls to 70%
    3. the distribution for n = 20 is skewed
    4. n = 20 adversely affects the location of the mean
    5. the variance is a biased estimate

22. A large lot of parts is rejected by your customer and found to be 20% defective. What is the probability that the lot would have been accepted by the following sampling plan: sample size = 10; accept if no defectives; reject if one or more defectives?
    1. .89
    2. .63
    3. .01
    4. .80
    5. .11

23. In performing an analysis of variance in a single factor experiment, a fundamental assumption which is made is that the:
    1. factor (column) means are equal
    2. factor (column) means are unequal
    3. column variances are equal
    4. column variances are significantly different

24. The distribution of a characteristic is negatively skewed. The sampling distribution of the mean for large samples is:
    1. negatively skewed
    2. approximately normal
    3. positively skewed
    4. bimodal
    5. Poisson

25. When an initial study is made of a repetitive industrial process for the purpose of setting up a Shewhart control chart, information on the following process characteristic is sought.
    1. process capability
    2. process performance
    3. process reliability
    4. process conformance
    5. process tolerance

26. You look at a process and note that the chart for averages has been in control. If the range suddenly and significantly increases, the mean will:
    1. always increase
    2. stay the same
    3. always decrease
    4. occasionally show out of control of either limit
    5. none of the above

27. A factorial experiment has been performed to determine the effect of factor A and Factor B on the strength of a part. An "F" test shows a significant interaction effect. This means that:
    1. either factor A or Factor B has a significant effect on strength
    2. both factor A and Factor B effect strength
    3. the effect of changing Factor B can be estimated only if the level of factor A is known
    4. neither factor A nor Factor B effect strength
    5. that strength will increase if factor A is increased while Factor B is held at a low level.

28. When using the Poisson as an approximation to the binomial the following conditions apply for the best approximation:
    1. larger sample size and larger fraction defective
    2. larger sample size and smaller fraction defective
    3. smaller sample size and larger fraction defective
    4. smaller sample size and smaller fraction defective

29. Your major product cannot be fully inspected without destruction. You have been requested to plan the inspection program, including some product testing, in the most cost-effective manner. You most probably will recommend that samples selected for the product verification be based upon:
    1. MIL-STD-105D, latest issue; attribute sampling
    2. MIL-STD-414, latest issue; variables sampling
    3. either answers 1 or 2 above will meet your criteria
    4. neither answers 1 nor 2 above will meet your criteria

30. In recent months, several quality problems have resulted from

apparent change in design specifications by engineering, including material substitutions. This has only come to light through Quality Engineering's failure analysis system. You recommend which of the following quality system provisions as the best corrective action:
1. establishing a formal procedure for initial design review
2. establishing a formal procedure for process control
3. establishing a formal procedure for specification change control (sometimes called an ECO or SCO system)
4. establishing a formal system for drawing and print control
5. establishing a formal material review (MRB) system

31. When a Quality Engineer wants parts removed from a line which is operating for tolerance checking, he should:
1. request the operator and/or supervisor to get them while he is observing
2. request the operator and/or supervisor to sample the line and bring them to his office
3. get the samples himself without notifying either the operator and/or supervisor
4. go out to the line, stop it himself, take the part, start it, and leave as quickly as possible

32. Source inspection should be employed when:
1. purchasing placed the order late and you want to help
2. manufacturing is screaming for the material and you want to help
3. you do not have appropriate gates and management won't buy them
4. source is more costly than receiving inspection but it reduces backlog in receiving
5. none of the above

33. A vendor quality control plan has been adopted; which of the following provisions would you advise top management to be the least effective?
1. product audits
2. source inspection
3. certificate of analysis
4. certificate of compliance
5. pre-award surveys

34. One of the major hazards in the material review board procedure is the tendency of the board to emphasize only the disposition function and to neglect the _____ _____ function.
1. statistical analysis
2. corrective action
3. material evaluation
4. tolerance review
5. manufacturing methods

35. The most desirable method of evaluating a supplier is:
1. history evaluation
2. survey evaluation
3. questionaire
4. discuss with quality manager on phone
5. all of the above

36. On the production floor, parts being produced measure .992 - 1.011. The specification requires the parts to be .995 - 1.005. Which of the following techniques would *not* be particularly useful in trying to improve and control the process?
1. pre-control
2. MIL-STD-105 charts
3. Multi-vari charts
4. $\overline{X}$ and R charts
5. machine capability analysis

37. The most important step in vendor certification is to:
1. obtain copies of vendor's handbook
2. familiarize vendor with quality requirements
3. analyze vendor's first shipment
4. visit the vendor's plant

38. The most important measure of outgoing quality needed by managers is product performance as viewed by:
1. the customer
2. the final inspector
3. production
4. marketing

39. Much managerial decision making is based on comparing actual performance with _____
1. personnel ratio
2. cost of operations
3. number of complaints
4. standards of performance

40. A technique whereby various product features are graded and

varying degrees of quality control applied is called:
1. zero defects
2. quality engineering
3. classification of characteristics
4. feature grading
5. nonsense — you cannot do it

41. Ultrasonic flaw detection instruments are calibrated using which the following types of standards?
1. NBS traceable time/voltage standards
2. natural flaws in the material being inspected
3. not calibrated since NBS traceable standards are not available
4. distance/amplitude reference blocks
5. artificial flaw transfer standards

42. Wear allowances on a "go" plug gage results in gages that are:
1. on the low limit of the specification
2. slightly larger diameter than the hi-limit of the specification
3. slightly smaller diameter than the low-limit of the specification
4. slightly larger diameter than the low-limit of the specification
5. on the high limit of the specification

43. A dial indicator nib must be perpendicular to measurement to avoid:
1. cosine error
2. axis error
3. profile error
4. configuration error

44. When considering whether to use radiographic or ultrasonic inspection to examine critical welds in thick materials, which of the following criteria is the best reason for this selection?
1. ultrasonic, since greater thicknesses can be prevented
2. radiography, since ultrasonic is less sensitive to porosity and inclusions
3. both, since the methods complement rather than supplant one another
4. both, since each is equally effective, the chance of missing a serious flaw is reduced

45. In the area for receiving inspection, which of the following items would not be in the inspection package?
1. purchase order
2. drawings to the latest revisions
3. drawings to the revisions of the purchase order
4. detailed inspection instructions

46. Which of the following pairs measure the same type of characteristics?

A) Pounds-Kelvin   D) PSI-Grams
B) BTU-Calorie   E) Fahrenheit-Hectare
C) Pound Force-Newton F) Acre-Grams

1. A, B, D, and F
2. A, C, and E
3. B and C
4. B, D, and F
5. A, C, E, and F

47. Calibration intervals should be adjusted when:
1. no defective product is reported as being erroneously accepted as a result of measurement errors
2. few instruments are scrapped out during calibration
3. the results of previous calibrations reflect few out of tolerance conditions during calibration
4. a particular characteristic on a gage is consistently found out of tolerance

48. A typical use for the optical comparator would be to measure:
1. surface finish
2. contours
3. depth of holes
4. diameters of internal grooves
5. all of the above

49. The primary advantage of the use of radio-isotopes, such as Cobalt 60 as compared to an X-ray generator, such as a betatron, is:
1. duration of radiation can be controlled by turning off the source
2. portability
3. the energy given off is heterogeneous, covering a wide range of wavelengths
4. the energy given off by the source stays constant with time

50. The gradual loss of sonic energy as the ultrasonic vibrations travel through the material is referred to as:
1. refraction
2. reproducibility
3. reflection
4. attenuation

5. diffraction

51. "Beauty Defects" can best be described for Inspection acceptance purposes by:
 1. simply stating such defects are unacceptable
 2. verbally describing rejection criteria
 3. leaving them up to the inspector
 4. establishing visual standards and/or samples describing the defects
 5. establishing written standards describing the defects

52. Which of the following is the symbol for surface finish requirements?
 1. λ
 2. M
 3. $\sqrt{}$
 4. M/S
 5. △

53. Quality cost analysis has shown that appraisal costs are apparently too high in relation to sales. Which of the following actions probably would *not* be considered in pursuing this problem?
 1. work sampling in inspection and test areas
 2. adding inspectors to reduce scrap costs
 3. pareto analysis of quality costs
 4. considering elimination of some test operations
 5. comparing appraisal costs to bases other than sales — for example direct labor, value added, etc.

54. Analyze the cost data below:

$	10,000	— equipment design
	150,000	— scrap
	180,000	— reinspection and retest
	45,000	— loss or disposition of surplus stock
	4,000	— vendor quality surveys
	40,000	— repair

Considering only the Quality Costs shown above, we might conclude that:
 1. prevention costs should be decreased
 2. internal failure costs can be decreased
 3. prevention costs are too low a proportion of the quality costs shown
 4. appraisal costs should be increased
 5. nothing can be concluded

55. This month's quality cost data collection shows the following:

Returned material processing	$	1,800
Adjustment of customer complaints		4,500
Rework and repair		10,700
Quality management salaries		25,000
Warranty replacement		54,500
Calibration and maintenance of test equip.		2,500
Inspection and testing		28,000

For your 'action' report to top management you select which one of the following as the percentage of *"External Failure"* to *"Total Quality Costs"* to show the true impact of field problems?
 1. 20%
 2. 55%
 3. 48%
 4. 24%
 5. 8%

56. You have been assigned as a quality engineer to a small company. The quality control manager desires some cost data and the accounting department reported that the following information is available. Cost accounts are production inspection, $14,185; test inspection, $4,264; procurement inspection, $2,198; shop labor, $141,698; shop rework, $1,402; first article, $675; engineering analysis (rework), $845; repair service (warrantee), $298; quality engineering, $2,175; design engineering salaries, $241,451; quality equipment, $18,745; training, $275; receiving laboratories, $385; underwriters laboratories, $1,200; installation service cost, $9,000; scrap, $1,182; and calibration service, $794.

What are the preventive costs?

 1. $3,727
 2. $23,701
 3. $23,026
 4. $3,295
 5. $2,450

57. Quality cost analysis has shown that appraisal costs are apparently too high in relation to sales. Which of the following actions probably would not be considered in pursuing this problem?
 1. work sampling in inspection and test areas.

2. adding inspectors to reduce scrap costs
3. pareto analysis of quality costs
4. considering elimination of some test operations
5. comparing appraisal costs to bases other than sales — for example, direct labor, value added, etc.

58. The percentages of total quality cost are distributed as follows:

Prevention	12%
Appraisal	28%
Internal Failure	40%
External Failure	20%

We conclude:
 1. We should invest more money in Prevention.
 2. Expenditures for Failures are excessive.
 3. The amount spent for Appraisal seems about right.
 4. Nothing.

59. One of the following is *not* a factor to consider in establishing quality information equipment cost:
 1. debugging cost
 2. amortization period
 3. design cost
 4. replacement parts and spares
 5. book cost

60. One method to control inspection costs even without a budget is by comparing _____ as a ratio to productive machine time to produce the product.
 1. product cost
 2. company profit
 3. inspection hours
 4. scrap material

61. A complete Quality Cost Reporting System would include which of the following as part of the quality cost?
 1. test time costs associated with installing the product at the customer's facility prior to turning the product over to the customer
 2. the salary of a product designer preparing a deviation authorization for material produced outside of design specifications
 3. cost of scrap
 4. all of the above
 5. none of the above

62. When prevention costs are increased, to pay for the right kind of engineering work in quality control, a reduction in the number of product defects occurs. This defect reduction means a substantial reduction in _____.
 1. appraisal costs
 2. operating costs
 3. prevention costs
 4. failure costs
 5. manufacturing costs

63. Which of the following techniques would not be used in a quality audit?
 1. select samples only from completed lots
 2. examine samples from viewpoint of critical customer
 3. audit only those items which have caused customer complaints
 4. use audit information in future design planning
 5. frequency of audit to depend on economic and quality requirements

64. During the pre-award survey at a potential key supplier, you discover the existence of a Quality Control Manual, this means:
 1. that a quality system has been developed
 2. that a quality system has been implemented
 3. that the firm is quality conscious
 4. that the firm has a quality manager
 5. all of the above

65. Which of the following quality system provisions is of the *least* concern when preparing an audit check list for the upcoming branch operation quality system audit:
 1. drawing and print control
 2. make-up of the MRB (material review board)
 3. engineering design change control
 4. control of special processes
 5. calibration of test equipment

66. You are requested by top management to establish an audit program of the quality systems in each branch plant of your firm. Which of the following schemes would you use in selecting the audit team to optimize continuity, direction, availability, and technology transfer?
 1. full time audit staff

2. all volunteer audit staff
3. the boss' son and son-in-law
4. hybrid audit staff (a proportion of answers 1 and 2 above)
5. any of the above will make an effective audit team

67. An audit will be viewed as a constructive service to the function which is audited when it:
1. is conducted by non-technical auditors
2. proposes corrective action for each item uncovered
3. furnishes enough detailed facts so the necessary action can be determined
4. is general enough to permit managerial intervention

68. Which of the following is not a responsibility of the auditor?
1. prepare a plan and checklist
2. report results to those responsible
3. investigate deficiencies for cause and define the corrective action that must be taken
4. follow up to see if the corrective action was taken
5. none of the above

69. Reliability testing of parts is performed to yield which of the following type of information?
1. application suitability
2. environmental capability
3. measurement of life characteristics
4. all of the above
5. none of the above

70. Failure mode, effect, and criticality analysis, (FMECA) is primarily for the purpose of:
1. learning as much about the item as possible after qualification test
2. determining the way an item will most likely fail to help obtain design and procedural safeguards against such failures
3. determining, by extensive analysis, the reliability of an item
4. determining the cause of a failure, by dissecting the item, to help obtain corrective action

71. According to the definition of reliability, performance over the expected or intended life is one criterion. In order to obtain a measurement for reliability, the actual life (t) must be compared to which of the following?
1. sampling of components
2. Test cycles (T_c)
3. Required life (T)
4. MTBF
5. probability of failures (P_x)

72. For a high compression aircraft air conditioning system, the MTBF is 100 hours. This mean life is allocated to four serial units comprising the total system. The unit failure rates are then weighted as follows:

$$w_1 = 0.1250 \qquad w_3 = 0.1875$$
$$w_2 = 0.2500 \qquad w_4 = 0.4375$$

Based upon the above data, indicate which of the following is the correct calculation for one of the units:
1. $\lambda_3 = 0.001875$
2. $\lambda_4 = 0.043570$
3. $\lambda_1 = 0.012500$
4. $\lambda_3 = 0.0001875$
5. $\lambda_2 = 0.002510$

73. The basic steps in any data processing system using computers generally are arranged in which of the following orders:
1. data input, storage and retrieval, processing and output.
2. collection, analysis, input and output.
3. evaluation, keypunch, processing and output.
4. recording, input, calculation and output.
5. keypunch, FORTRAN programming, output.

74. When planning a system for processing quality data or for keeping inspection and other quality records, the first step should be to:
1. depict the system in a flow chart
2. hire a statistician
3. investigate applicable data processing equipment
4. determine the cost of operating the system
5. start coding your input data

75. The management team is establishing priorities to attack a serious quality problem. You are requested to establish a data collection system to direct this attack. You use which of these general management rules to support your recommendations as to the quantity of data required:
1. You have compared the incremental cost of additional data with the value of the information obtained and stopped when they are equal.
2. Your decision corresponds to the rules applicable to management decisions for other factors of production.
3. Your decision is based upon the relationship between value and cost.
4. All of the above.

76. Computer information processing can become available to a Quality Engineer through the use of:
1. a terminal and time sharing agreement
2. a batch processing system in which data is brought to a central area for processing
3. an in-house system with applicable software
4. all of the above

77. In a visual inspection situation, one of the best ways to minimize deterioration of the quality level is to:
1. re-train the inspector frequently
2. add variety to the task
3. have a program of frequent eye exams
4. have frequent breaks
5. have a standard to compare against a part of the operation

78. Which of the following methods used to improve employe efficiency and promote an atmosphere conducive to quality and profit is the most effective in the long run?
1. offering incentives such as bonus, praise, profit sharing, etc.
2. strict discipline to reduce mistakes, idleness, and sloppiness.
3. combination of incentive and discipline to provide both reward for excellence and punishment for inferior performance.
4. building constructive attitudes through development of realistic quality goals relating to both company and employe success
5. all of the above provided emphasis is placed on attitude motivation, with incentive and discipline used with utmost caution.

79. The Quality Engineer should be concerned with the human factors of a new piece of in-house manufacturing equipment as well as its operational effects because it:
1. may speed the line to the point where a visual operator inspection is impossible.
2. may require the operator's undivided attention at the controls so the product cannot be fully seen
3. may remove an operator formerly devoting some portion of tir to inspection
4. all of the above

80. The famous Hawthorne study provided which of the following clinical evidence regarding the factors that can increase work group productivity?
1. Attention and recognition is more important than working conditions.
2. Productivity did not change significantly under any of the test conditions
3. Informal group pressures set a production "goal."
4. People with higher capabilities are bored with routine jobs.
5. Work station layout is critical to higher productivity.

1. Attention and recognition is more important than working conditions.
2. Productivity did not change significantly under any of the test conditions.
3. Informal group pressures set a production "goal."
4. People with higher capabilities are bored with routine jobs.
5. Work station layout is critical to higher productivity.

CQE EXAM BIBLIOGRAPHY

Books Covering More Than One Subject Area
On The Quality Engineering Certification Examination

1. Dixon, W.J., and Massey, F.J., *Introduction to Statistic Analysis,* 3rd Edition, McGraw-Hill Book Company, 1969.
2. Feigenbaum, A.V., *Total Quality Control,* McGraw-Hill Book Co., Inc., New York, New York, 1961.
3. Hansen, B.L., *Quality Control: Theory and Applications,* Prentice-Hall, Inc., Englewood Cliffs, New Jersey, 1963.
4. Hayes, G.E., *Quality Assurance: Management & Technology,* Charger Productions, Inc., Capistrano Beach, California, 1974.

5. Juran, J.M., *Quality Control Handbook*, 3rd Edition, McGraw-Hill Book Company, Inc., New York, New York, 1974.
6. Juran, J.M., and Gryna, F.M., Jr., *Quality Planning and Analysis*, McGraw-Hill Book Co., Inc., New York, New York, 1970.
7. Miller, I., and Freund, J.E., *Probability and Statistics for Engineers*, 2nd Edition, Prentice-Hall, Inc., Englewood Cliffs, New Jersey, 1977.
8. ASQC "Glossary and Tables for Statistical Quality Control," Milwaukee, Wisconsin, 1973.
9. Ott, Ellis R., *Process Quality Control*, McGraw-Hill Book Co., Inc., New York, New York, 1975.
10. Hayes, Glenn E., and Romig, Henry G., *Modern Quality Control*, Bruce, Encino, California, 1977.

References More Specialized To The Subject Area

I. Fundamental Concepts of Probability, Statistical Quality Control, and Design of Experiments

Fundamental Concepts of Probability and Statistics

1. Freund, J.E., *Modern elementary Statistics*, 3rd Edition, Prentice-Hall, Inc., Englewood Cliffs, New Jersey, 1967.
2. Berry, D.A., Lindgren, B.W., and McElrath, G.W., *Introduction to Probability and Statistics*, 4th Edition, The MacMillan Co., New York, New York, 1978.
3. Rickmers, A.D., and todd, H.N., *Statistics, An Introduction*, McGraw-Hill Book Co., New York, New York, 1967.
4. Spiegel, M.R., *Statistics*, McGraw-Hill Book Co., New York, New York, (Schaum Outline Series), 1967.
5. Burr, I.W., *Applied Statistical Methods*, Academic Press, New York, New York, 1974.
6. Hine, J., and Wetherill, *A Programmed Text in Statistics*, Halsted Press (Division of John Wiley & Sons, Inc.), New York, New York, 1975.

Statistical Quality Control

1. ASQC Standard A-1, (ANSI Std. Z1.5-1971), "Definitions, Symbols Formulas, and Tables for Control Charts;" ASQC Standard A-2, (ANSI Std. Z1.6-1971), "Definitions and Symbols for Acceptance Sampling by Attributes;" ASQC Standard A-3, (ANSI Std. Z1.7-1971), "Glossary of General Terms Used in Quality Control," Milwaukee, Wisconsin, 1971.
2. Burr, I.W., *Statistical Quality Control Methods*, Marcel Dekker, Inc., New York, New York, 1976.
3. Dodge, H.F., and Romig, H.G., *Sampling Inspection Tables, Single and Double Sampling*, 2nd Edition, John Wiley and Sons, New York, New York, 1959.
4. Enrick, N.L., and Mottley, H.E., "Manufacturing Quality Control," 2nd Edition, ASQC, Milwaukee, Wisconsin.
5. Grant, E.L., and Leavenworth, R.S., *Statistical Quality Control*, 4th Edition, McGraw-Hill Book Co., Inc., New York, New York, 1972.
6. State University of Iowa Section, ASQC, "Quality Control Training Manual," 2nd Edition, 1965.
7. U.S. Department of Defense, MIL-STD-105D, "Sampling Procedures and Tables for Inspection by Variables," Government Printing Office, Washington, D.C., June 11, 1957.
9. Small, B.B., et al, "Statistical Quality Control Handbook," 2nd Edition, Western Electric Company, New York, New York, 1958.

Experimental Design

1. Davies, O.L., *Design and Analysis of Industrial Experiments*, 2nd Edition, Hafner Publishing Co., New York, New York, 1965.
2. Enrick, N.L., and Mottley, H.E., "Manufacturing Improvement Through Experimentation," ASQC, Milwaukee, Wisconsin, 1968.
3. Fisher, R.A., *The Design of Experiments*, Hafner Publishing co., New York, New York, 1954.
4. Hicks, C.R., *Fundamental Concepts in the Design of Experiments*, 2nd Edition, Holt, Rinehart, and Winston, New York, New York, 1973.

II. Quality Planning, Management, and Product Liability

1. "Procurement Quality Control," Vendor-Vendee Handbook, ASQC, 2nd Edition, Milwaukee, Wisconsin 1976.
2. "How to Conduct a Supplier Survey," ASQC, Milwaukee, Wisconsin, 1977.
3. Enrick, N.L., and Mottley, H.E., "Manufacturing Quality Control," 2nd Edition, ASQC, Milwaukee, Wisconsin, 1967.

4. Juran, J.M., *Managerial Breakthrough*, McGraw-Hill Book Co., Inc., New York, New York, 1964.
5. "Quality Control and Reliability Management," Training Manual, ASQC, Milwaukee, Wisconsin, 1969.
6. ASQC Standard C-1, (ANSI Std. Z1.8-1971), "Specification of General Requirements for a Quality Program," Milwaukee, Wisconsin, 1971.
7. "Matrix of Nuclear Quality Assurance Program Requirements," ASQC, Milwaukee, Wisconsin, 1976.
8. Proceedings — "Product Liability Prevention Conferences," 70-77, New Jersey Institute of Technology, Newark, New Jersey. Annuals 1970-1977.
9. Bases, A.L., Gray, I., Martin, C.H., and Sternberg, A., *Product Liability: A Management Response*, AMA, New York, New York, 1975.

III. Metrology, Inspection, and Testing

1. Busch, T., *Fundamentals of Dimensional Metrology*, Wilkie Brothers Foundation, Delmar Publishers, Inc., 2nd Edition, Albany, New York, 1965.
2. Convair Division, General Dynamics Corporation, PI-4 Series of Training Handbooks, San Diego, California.
3. Kennedy, C.W., *Inspection and Gaging*, 2nd Edition, The Industrial Press, New York, New York, 1951.
4. Manufacturers' literature (Federal Products, Brown & Sharpe, Starrett, etc.)
5. Michelon, L.C., *Industrial Inspection Methods*, revised Edition, Harper & Row., New York, New York, 1950.
6. ASTM, "Basic Principles of Sensory Evaluation," STP 433, 1968.
7. ASTM, "Manual on Sensory Testing Methods," STP 434, 1968.
8. MIL-HDBK-52, "Evaluation of Contractors Calibration Systems," (MIL-D-45662), U.S. Government Printing Office, Washington, D.C.
9. ASM, "Nondestructive Inspection and Quality Control," *Metals Handbook*, Vol. II, Metals Park, Ohio, 1976.
10. "Introduction to Nondestructive Testing," ASQC, Inspector's Handbook Series, Milwaukee, Wisconsin, 1978.
11. "Interlaboratory Testing Techniques," ASQC, Milwaukee, Wisconsin, 1978.

IV. Quality Cost Analysis

1. "Quality Costs — What and How," ASQC, 2nd Edition, Milwaukee, Wisconsin, 1971.
2. Transactions 22nd-32nd Annual Technical Conferences, ASQC, Milwaukee, Wisconsin, 1968-1978.
3. Information-Special Report, "How QC Can Boost Performance and Cut Costs," Prentice-Hall, Englewood Cliffs, New Jersey.
4. "Guide for Reducing Quality Costs," ASQC, Milwaukee, Wisconsin, 1977.

V. Quality Auditing

1. Ogden, J.E., "Product Quality Audit," Booklet X7-2776/201, Autonetics Division, Rockwell International Corporation, (reprinted, ASQC/ETI - 1973).
2. Johnson, L.M., *Quality Assurance Program Evaluation*, Stockton-Doty Trade Press, Inc., Whittier, California, 1970.
3. MIL-HDBK-50, "Evaluations of Contractors Quality Programs," (MIL-Q-9858), U.S. Government Printing Office, Washington, D.C.
4. MIL-HDBK-51, "Evaluations of Contractors Inspection Systems," (MIL-I-45208), U.S. Government Printing Office, Washington, D.C.
5. "Procurement Quality Control," Handbook of Recommended Practices, 2nd Edition, ASQC, Milwaukee, Wisconsin, 1976.
6. Convair Division, General Dynamics Corporation, PI-3 Series of Training Handbooks, San Diego, California.
7. "How to Conduct a Supplier Survey," ASQC, Milwaukee, Wisconsin, 1977.

VI. Reliability, Maintainability, and Product Safety

1. ARINC Research Corporation, (William H. Von Alven, Editor), *Reliability Engineering*, Prentice-Hall, Inc., Englewood Cliffs, New Jersey, 1964.
2. Bazovsky, I., *Reliability Theory and Practice*, Prentice-Hall, Inc., Englewood Cliffs, New Jersey, 1961.
3. Calabro, S.R., *Reliability Principles and Practices*, McGraw-Hill Book Co., Inc., New York, New York, 1962.

4. Goldman, A.S., and Slattery, T.B., *Maintainability: A Major Element of System Effectiveness,* John Wiley & Sons, Inc., 2nd Edition, New York, New York, June, 1967.
5. Ireson, W. Grant, (Editor), *Reliability Handbook,* McGraw-Hill Book Co., Inc., New York, New York, 1966.
6. Lloyd D.K., and Lipow, M., *Reliability and Management, Methods and Mathematics,* 2nd Edition, by authors, Redondo Beach, California, 1977.
7. Pieruschka, E., *Principles of Reliability,* Prentice-Hall, Inc., Englewood Cliffs, New Jersey, 1963.
8. "Reliability Training Text," 2nd Edition, ASQC and Institute of Radio Engineers, Milwaukee, Wisconsin, 1963.
9. "Reliability Reporting Guide," ASQC, Milwaukee, Wisconsin, 1977.
10. Hammer, Willie, *Handbook of System and Product Safety,* Prentice-Hall, Inc., Englewood Cliffs, New Jersey, 1972.
11. Brown, David B., *System Analysis and Design for Safety,* Prentice-Hall, Inc., Englewood Cliffs, New Jersey, 1976.
12. Rodgers, William P., *Introduction to System Safety Engineering,* Wiley & Sons, Inc., 1971.
13. "Company Product Safety and Product Loss Prevention Program — Guidelines for Management," National Safety Council, (includes Consumer Product Safety Act, 1972 and guidelines for in-house product safety audit).

VII. Quality Information Systems

1. Awad, E.M., *Business Data Processing,* 2nd Edition, Prentice-Hall, Inc., Englewood Cliffs, New Jersey, 1968.
2. Data Processing Management Association, *Automatic Data Processing: Principles and Procedures,* Prentice-Hall, Inc., Englewood Cliffs, New Jersey, 1966.
3. Elliot, C.O., and Wasley, R.S., *Business Information Processing Systems,* Richard D. Irwin, Inc., Homewood, Illinois, 1965.
4. Davis, Gordon B., *Introduction to Electronic Computer,* 2nd Edition, McGraw-Hill Book Co., Inc., New York, New York, 1971.
5. Martin, E.W., *Electronics Data Processing: An Introduction,* Revised Edition, Richard D. Irwin, Inc., Homewood, Illinois, 1965.
6. Freund, J.E., and Williams, F.S., *Modern Business Statistics,* (pp. 338-473), Prentice-Hall, Inc., Englewood Cliffs, New Jersey, 1965.
7. "Quality Costs — What and How," ASQC, 2nd Edition, Milwaukee, Wisconsin, 1971.
8. Foster, Richard A., *Introduction to Software Quality Assurance,* Third Edition, 5411 Entrada Cedras, San Jose, California, 95123, 1975.
9. "Reliability Reporting Guide," ASQC, Milwaukee, Wisconsin, 1977.

VIII. Motivation and Human Factors

1. Argyris, C., *Personality and Organization,* Harper & Row, 1957.
2. Harris, D.H., and Chaney, F.B., *Human Factors in Quality Assurance,* John Wiley & Sons, Inc., New York, New York, 1969.
3. Herzberg, F., *Work and the Nature of Man,* World Publishing Co., 1966.
4. Maslow, A., "A Theory of Human Motivation," Psychological Review, Volume 50, pp. 370-396.
5. McGregor, D., *Human Side of the Enterprise,* McGraw-Hill Book Co., Inc., New York, New York, 1960.
6. "Quality Motivation Workbook" ASQC, Milwaukee, Wisconsin, 1967, (reprint 1978, bibliography added).
7. Tiffin & McCormick, *Industrial Psychology,* Prentice-Hall, Inc., Englewood Cliffs, New Jersey, 1965.
8. Stok, T.L., *The Worker and Quality Control,* Bureau of Industrial Relations, University of Michigan, Ann Arbor, Michigan, 1965.
9. "QC Circles: Applications, Tools, and Theory," ASQC, Milwaukee, Wisconsin, 1976.

ANSWERS

Applications

#	Ans	#	Ans
1.	1	58.	4
2.	3	59.	5
3.	4	60.	3
4.	3	61.	4
5.	4	62.	4
6.	3	63.	3
7.	2	64.	1
8.	2	65.	2
9.	2	66.	4
10.	3	67.	3
11.	4	68.	3
12.	5	69.	4
13.	2	70.	2
14.	4	71.	3
15.	4	72.	1
16.	4	73.	1
17.	2	74.	1
18.	3	75.	4
19.	2	76.	4
20.	2	77.	5
21.	2	78.	5
22.	5	79.	4
23.	3	80.	1
24.	2		
25.	1		
26.	4		
27.	3		
28.	2		
29.	2		
30.	3		
31.	1		
32.	3		
33.	4		
34.	2		
35.	1		
36.	2		
37.	2		
38.	1		
39.	4		
40.	3		
41.	4		
42.	4		
43.	1		
44.	3		
45.	2		
46.	3		
47.	4		
48.	2		
49.	2		
50.	4		
51.	4		
52.	3		
53.	2		
54.	3		
55.	3		
56.	5		
57.	2		

Principles

#	Ans	#	Ans
1.	2	33.	3
2.	5	34.	5
3.	4	35.	5
4.	1	36.	3
5.	5	37.	4
6.	2	38.	5
7.	2	39.	4
8.	2	40.	1
9.	1	41.	2
10.	3	42.	3
11.	1	43.	1
12.	2	44.	3
13.	2	45.	3
14.	2	46.	2
15.	3	47.	4
16.	1	48.	2
17.	4	49.	1
18.	2	50.	3
19.	1	51.	1
20.	1	52.	4
21.	2	53.	4
22.	4	54.	4
23.	4	55.	3
24.	5	56.	3
25.	4	57.	3
26.	2	58.	3
27.	4	59.	5
28.	4	60.	3
29.	2	61.	4
30.	1	62.	3
31.	4	63.	2
32.	4	64.	3
		65.	5
		66.	3
		67.	5
		68.	5
		69.	1
		70.	3
		71.	4
		72.	5
		73.	2
		74.	2
		75.	4
		76.	1
		77.	2
		78.	5
		79.	4
		80.	1
		81.	3
		82.	4
		83.	5
		84.	3
		85.	4
		86.	4
		87.	4
		88.	3
		89.	5
		90.	4

APPLICATIONS

1. Given that random samples of process A produced 10 defective and 30 good units, while process B produced 5 defectives out of 60 units. Using the chi-square test, what is the probability that the observed value of chi-square could result, under the hypothesis that both processes are operating at the same quality level?
   a. Less than 5 percent.
   b. *Between 5 percent and 10 percent.**
   c. Greater than 10 percent.
   d. 50 percent.
2. How many degrees of freedom should you use in the above problem?
   a. *1*
   b. 2
   c. 3
   d. 4
3. On the basis of the data in the previous problem, what would you conclude?
   a. *Nothing. The facts involving the consequences of a wrong decision are unknown.*
   b. The two processes are comparable.
   c. The two processes are significantly different.
   d. Reject the null hypothesis.
4. Color can be described as:
   a. One dimensional.
   b. Two dimensional.
   c. *Three dimensional.*
   d. Photometric.
5. Wear allowance on a go plug gage permits gages to be:
   a. Slightly smaller in diameter than the low limit of specification
   b. *Slightly larger in diameter than the low limit of specification*
   c. Right on the low limit of specification.
   d. Slightly larger in diameter than the high limit of specification.
6. To insure success of a quality audit program, the most important activity for a quality supervisor is:
   a. Setting up audit frequency.
   b. Maintenance of a checking procedure to see that all required audits are performed.
   c. *Getting corrective action as a result of audit findings.*
   d. Checking that the audit procedure is adequate and complete.
7. Measurement gaging is preferable to go-no-go gaging in a quality characteristic because:
   a. It is more scientific.
   b. *It provides the most information per piece inspected.*
   c. It requires greater skills.
   d. It requires a larger sample than gaging does.
8. Characteristics of a good Incoming Inspection Department are:
   a. Written and visual quality standards.
   b. Proper inspection equipment and gages.
   c. Inspector knowledge of sampling techniques.
   d. *All of the above.*
9. The technology for predicting human reliability in production processes:
   a. Is inevitably correlated with monetary rewards.
   b. Is represented by the many motivation programs in effect.
   c. *Is still in the developmental stages.*
   d. Is based on the determination of the workmanship error rate.
10. In planning for quality, an important consideration at the start is:
    a. The relation of the total cost of quality to the net sales.
    b. *The establishment of a company quality policy or objective.*
    c. Deciding precisely how much money is to be spent.
    d. The selling of the quality program to top management.
11. The sample size for a product quality audit should be:
    a. Based on MIL-STD-105D.
    b. Based on the lot size.
    c. A stated percentage of production.
    d. *Very small.*
12. Which of the following nondestructive testing methods is best for rapid inspection of ½ in. diameter carbon steel rod one foot long for surface cracks?
    a. Radiography.
    b. Ultrasonic.
    c. *Magnetic particle.*
    d. Liquid penetrant.

13. To measure an angle on a work piece the most accurate method would involve the use of:
    a. A sine-bar.
    b. A set of plastic triangles.
    c. A bevel protractor.
    d. None of the above.
14. Who has the initial responsibility for manufactured product quality?
    a. The inspector.
    b. The vice president.
    c. *The operator.*
    d. The quality manager.
15. What type of gaging instrument would you use to determine the fractional part of an inch that can be read by multiplying the denominator of the finest subdivision on the scale by the total number of divisions on the second scale?
    a. *Vernier.*
    b. Micrometer.
    c. Comparator.
    d. Demonimeter.
16. Given the following results obtained from a fixed factor randomized block designed experiment in which the production outputs of three machines A, B, C are compared:

A	4	8	5	7	6
B	2	0	1	-2	4
C	-3	1	-2	-1	0

    How many degrees of freedom are used to compute the error variance?
    a. 2
    b. 3
    c. *12*
    d. 14
17. What is the critical value of F at 0.05 risk for the previous problem?
    a. *3.89*
    b. 4.75
    c. 3.49
    d. 4.60
18. What is the sum of squares for the error term in the previous problem?
    a. 170
    b. 130
    c. *40*
    d. 14
19. The purpose of such an experiment described in the previous problem is to compare:
    a. The output variances of the three machines.
    b. The variance of the machines against the error.
    c. *The output averages of the three machines.*
    d. The process capabilities of the three machines.
20. The term "random access" identifies information stored:
    a. *Where all parts of it are designed to be equally accessible when needed.*
    b. Someplace inside a computer, whose address only the computer's scanning device can locate.
    c. Outside a computer, so it has to be sought by humans rather than electronically.
    d. In the special part of the processing unit for temporary storage only.
21. Assume a large lot contains exactly 4 percent defective items. Using the Poisson distribution, what is the probability that a random sample of 50 items will *not* reflect the true lot quality?
    a. 27%
    b. *73%*
    c. 82%
    d. 67%
22. When setting up a sorting operation for a visual defect, which one of the following is most important?
    a. The importance of the defect
    b. Whether the operator or inspector does the job.
    c. The percent defective estimated to be in the lot.
    d. *The quality standard.*
23. A device used to measure viscosity or consistency is
    a. Viscosimeter.
    b. Farinograph
    c. Consistometer.
    d. *All of above.*

---

*Correct answers are printed in italic type.

24. Which one of the following tasks has been shown to have the most incentive or motivational value to the quality engineer?
   a. Attend defect control meetings.
   b. Document action taken on special problems.
   c. *Investigate product quality problems.*
   d. Initiate corrective action to solve nonroutine problems.

25. When planning the specifications for product quality in the so-called "mechanical" industries:
   a. Market research helps to establish economic tolerances.
   b. Quality control develops products possessing qualities which meet customer needs.
   c. Product research issues official product specifications.
   d. *Product design assumes prime responsibility for establishing economic tolerances.*

26. In the so-called "process" industries:
   a. Quality control has some responsibility in choosing the process.
   b. Quality control may help to establish process tolerances.
   c. Process development issues process specifications.
   d. *All of the above.*

27. Shewhart $\overline{X}$ control charts are designed with which one of the following objectives?
   a. Reduce sample size.
   b. Fix risk of accepting poor product.
   c. *Decide when to hunt for causes of variation.*
   d. Establish an acceptable quality level.

28. If the probability of a success on a single trial is 0.2, and 3 trials are performed, what is the probability of at least one success?
   a. 0.008
   b. 0.384
   c. *0.488*
   d. 0.600

29. A process is acceptable if its standard deviation is not greater than 1.0. A sample of four items yields the values 52, 56, 53, 55. In order to determine if the process be accepted or rejected, the following statistical test should be used:
   a. t-test.
   b. *Chi-square test.*
   c. Z-test.
   d. None of the above.

30. When planning the quality aspects of packing and shipping, it is *not* usual that the:
   a. Product design department specify packaging and shipping procedures.
   b. Shipping department conduct packing and shipping operations.
   c. *Inspection department determine package specifications.*
   d. Inspection department check the adequacy of packing and shipping operations.

31. If the distribution of defectives among various lots is found to follow the laws of chance, we can conclude that:
   a. *The product was well mixed before dividing into lots.*
   b. The manufacturing process is not predictable.
   c. All lots should be accepted.
   d. None of the above is true.

32. When purchasing materials from vendors, it is sometimes advantageous to choose vendors whose prices are higher because:
   a. Materials which cost more can be expected to be better, and "you get what you pay for."
   b. Such vendors may become obligated to bestow special favors.
   c. Such a statement is basically incorrect. Always buy at lowest bid price.
   d. *The true cost of purchased materials, which should include items such as sorting inspection, contacting vendors and production delays, may be lower.*

33. In a scanning type inspection task, inspection accuracy is likely to be greater if:
   a. The product moves toward the inspector rather than laterally past him.
   b. The inspector search the product, area by area, for all types of defects rather than the entire product for the type of defect at a time.
   c. The magnification is increased.
   d. *The product is scanned while it is stationary rather than while it is moving.*

34. In which one of the following is the use of an $\overline{X}$ and R chart liable to be helpful as a tool to control a process?
   a. The machine capability is wider than the specification.
   b. The machine capability is equal to the specification.
   c. *The machine capability is somewhat smaller than the specification.*
   d. The machine capability is very small compared to the specification.

35. The basic concept of MIL-STD-105D sampling tables and procedures is that:
   a. Poor product is accepted infrequently.
   b. Good product is accepted rarely.
   c. Poor product is accepted consistently.
   d. *Good product is accepted most of the time.*

36. In acceptance sampling, the probability of accepting a rejectable lot is called:
   a. *Beta.*
   b. AQL.
   c. Alpha.
   d. LTPD.

37. When performing calculations on sample data:
   a. The cumulative relative frequency graph that is often used is called a histogram.
   b. Rounding the data has no effect on the mean and standard deviation.
   c. Coding the data has no effect on the mean and standard deviation.
   d. *Coding and rounding affect both the mean and standard deviation.*

38. When analyzing quality costs, a helpful method for singling out the highest cost contributors is:
   a. A series of interviews with the line foreman.
   b. *The application of the Pareto theory.*
   c. An audit of budget variances.
   d. The application of break-even and profit volume analysis.

39. One of the most important techniques in making a training program effective is to:
   a. *Give people meaningful measures of performance.*
   b. Transmit all of the information that is even remotely related to the function.
   c. Set individual goals instead of group goals.
   d. Concentrate only on developing knowledge and skills needed to do a good job.

40. The Dodge-Romig sampling tables for AOQL protection:
   a. *Require sorting of rejected lots.*
   b. Are the same in principle as the MIL-STD-105D tables.
   c. Do not depend upon the process average.
   d. Require larger samples than MIL-STD-105D for equivalent quality assurances.

41. EVOP should be used:
   a. When there is a manufacturing problem.
   b. When a process is not in statistical control.
   c. When an experimenter first begins working on a new product.
   d. *When a process is producing satisfactory material.*

42. Three parts are additive in an assembly. Their design specifications for length and tolerance are 0.240 ±0.006, 0.3200 ±0.0006, and 1.360 ±0.003 respectively. Assume that each of the distributions is normal. Combine these dimensions statistically to give a final length and tolerance to three decimal places.
   a. 1.360 ±0.006
   b. 0.799 ±0.565
   c. 0.640 ±0.010
   d. *1.920 ±0.007*

43. If a process is out of control, the theoretical probability that four consecutive points on an $\overline{X}$ chart will fall on the same side of the mean is:
   a. *Unknown.*
   b. $(\frac{1}{2})^4$
   c. $2 \cdot (\frac{1}{2})^4$
   d. $\frac{1}{2} \cdot (\frac{1}{2})^4$

44. An incomplete block design may be especially suitable when:
   a. There is missing data.
   b. There is need for fractional replication.
   c. *It may not be possible to apply all treatments in every block.*
   d. There is need to estimate the parameters during the experimentation.

45. A cost estimate associated with average outgoing quality protection is usually determined from the:
   a. *Average total inspection.*
   b. Average outgoing quality.
   c. Average sample size.
   d. Acceptable quality limit.

46. Using a 10 percent sample of each lot, with an acceptance number of zero, regardless of lot size:
   a. Results in a constant level of protection against bad product.

b. Assures a constant producer's risk.
c. *Abdicates the responsibility for pre-determining quality requirements.*
d. Provides an AQL of zero and an LTPD of 10 percent.

47. Estimate the variance of the population from which the following sample data came: 22, 18, 17, 20, 21.
    a. *4.3*
    b. 2.1
    c. 1.9
    d. 5.0

48. The operating characteristic (OC) curve of an acceptance sampling plan:
    a. Demonstrates how the plan will reject all of the lots worse than the AQL.
    b. *Shows the ability of the plan to distinguish between good and bad lots.*
    c. Shows the relative cost of sampling for various levels of quality.
    d. Demonstrates the advantages of double sampling over single sampling.

49. The quality cost of writing instructions and operating procedures for inspection and testing should be charged to:
    a. Appraisal costs.
    b. Internal failure costs.
    c. *Prevention costs.*
    d. External failure costs.

50. In a normal distribution, what is the area under the curve between +0.7 and +1.3 standard deviation units?
    a. 0.2903
    b. 0.7580
    c. 0.2580
    d. *0.1452*

51. A useful tool to determine when to investigate excessive variation in a process is:
    a. MIL-STD-105D.
    b. *Control chart.*
    c. Dodge-Romig AOQL sampling table.
    d. Process capability study.

52. Calculate the standard deviation of the following complete set of data: 52, 20, 24, 31, 35, 42.
    a. *10.8*
    b. 11.8
    c. 12.8
    d. 13.8

53. It is generally considered desirable that quality audit reports be:
    a. Stated in terms different from those of the function being audited.
    b. *Simple but complete.*
    c. Sent to the general manager in all cases.
    d. Quantitative in all cases.

54. Establishing the quality policy for the company is typically the responsibility of:
    a. Marketing department.
    b. *Top management.*
    c. Quality control.
    d. Customer.

55. Two balance scales are to be compared by weighing the same five items on each scale, yielding the following results:

	Item #1	#2	#3	#4	#5
Scale A	110	99	112	85	99
Scale B	112	101	113	88	101

    The sharpest test comparing mean effects is obtained by using which one of the following:
    a. *Paired data test of significance with 4 degrees of freedom.*
    b. $t = \dfrac{\overline{X}_A - \overline{X}_B}{S_p / \sqrt{n}}$ for 8 degrees of freedom.
    c. Analysis of variance for randomized blocks.
    d. Determining the correlation coefficient r.

56. "Determine the flux meter reading of the part per specification." This inspection instruction violates which of the following guiding principles:
    a. A specific objective should be established for each instruction.
    b. Only necessary words should be used.
    c. *The correct inspection method should be stated in operational terms.*
    d. All of the above.

57. A value of 0.9973 refers to the probability that:
    a. The process is in control.
    b. A correct decision will be made as to control or lack of control of the process.

c. The process is unstable.
d. *A point will fall inside three-sigma limits for an $\overline{X}$ chart if process is in control.*

58. A chart for number of defects is called:
    a. np chart.
    b. p chart.
    c. $\overline{X}$ chart.
    d. *c chart.*

59. When considering EVOP as a statistical tool:
    a. A change in the means indicates that we are using the wrong model.
    b. An external estimate of the experiment error is necessary.
    c. *EVOP may be extended beyond the two level factorial case.*
    d. We are limited to one response variable at a time. A new EVOP should be run for each response.

60. The Dodge-Romig tables for AOQL protection are designed to provide:
    a. Minimum average sampling costs.
    b. Maximum protection against poor material.
    c. Maximum risk of accepting good lots.
    d. *Minimum average total inspection for a given process average.*

61. Each value below is the number of defects found in a group of five subassemblies inspected.

77	61	59	22	54
64	49	54	92	22
75	65	41	89	40
93	45	87	55	33
45	77	40	25	20

    Assume that a c chart is to be used for future production. Calculate the preliminary three-sigma control limits from the above data:
    a. 82.5, 28.9
    b. 15.6, 6.6
    c. 65.7, 45.7
    d. *78.2, 33.2*

62. Refering to the data in the preceding question, if points are outside of the control limits and we wish to set up a control chart for future production:
    a. More data are needed.
    b. *Discard those points falling outside the control limits, for which you can identify an assignable cause, and revise the limits.*
    c. Check with production to determine the true process capability.
    d. Discard those points falling outside the control limits and revise the limits.

63. Included as a "prevention quality cost" would be:
    a. *Salaries of personnel engaged in the design of measurement and control equipment that is to be purchased.*
    b. Capital equipment purchased.
    c. Training costs of instructing plant personnel to achieve production standards.
    d. Sorting of nonconforming material which will delay or stop production.

64. The modern concept of budgeting quality costs is to:
    a. Budget each of the four segments: prevention, appraisal, internal and external failure.
    b. Concentrate on external failures; they are important to the business since they represent customer acceptance.
    c. *Establish budget for reducing the total of the quality costs.*
    d. Reduce expenditures on each segment.

65. The percentages of total quality cost are distributed as follows:

Prevention	2%
Appraisal	33%
Internal Failure	35%
External Failure	30%

    We can conclude:
    a. Expenditures for failures are excessive.
    b. *Nothing.*
    c. We should invest more money in prevention.
    d. The amount spent for appraisal seems about right.

66. Specifying a tolerance by +0.000, -0.001 is known as:
    a. Bilateral tolerance.
    b. Limit dimensioning.
    c. Manufacturing limits.
    d. *Unilateral tolerance.*

67. Component 1 has an exponential failure rate of 3×10^{-4} failures per hour. Component 2 normally is distributed with a mean of 600 hours and standard deviation of 200 hours. Assuming independence, calculate the reliability of the system after 200 hours.

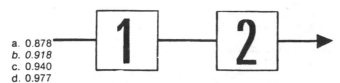

a. 0.878
b. 0.918
c. 0.940
d. 0.977

68. The main objection of designed experimentation in an industrial environment is:
    a. Obtaining more information for 'ess cost than can be obtained by traditional experimentation.
    b. *Getting excessive scrap as a result of choosing factor levels that are too extreme.*
    c. Verifying that one factor at a time is a most economical way to proceed.
    d. Obtaining data and then deciding what to do with it.

69. Using the range method, calculate the machine capability standard deviation to nearest 0.0001 of the following:

8 A.M.	9 A.M.	10 A.M.	11 A.M.
0.001	0.003	0.001	0.005
-0.001	0.004	-0.002	0.006
0.003	0.003	-0.003	0.005
0.002	0.004	0.002	0.005
0.001	0.002	0.000	0.006

    a. 0.0024
    b. 0.0470
    c. *0.0013*
    d. 0.0030

70. The purpose of a written inspection procedure is to:
    a. Provide answers to inspection questions.
    b. Let the operator know what the inspector is doing.
    c Fool-proof the inspection function.
    d. *Standardize methods and procedures of inspectors.*

71. The smallest size a 3-in. micrometer can measure is:
    a. 3-in.
    b. *2 in.*
    c. 1 in.
    d. 2.5 in.

72. Studies have shown that the most effective communications method for transferring information is:
    a. Oral only.
    b. Written only.
    c. *Combined written and oral.*
    d. Bulletin board.

73. Maintainability of an equipment may be measured in terms of:
    a. Maintenance dollar cost.
    b. Maintenance manhours.
    c. Repair time.
    d. *All of the above.*

74. Assume that the cost data available to you for a certain period are limited to the following:
    $ 20,000 - Final test
    350,000 - Field warranty costs
    170,000 - Reinspection and retest
    45,000 - Loss on disposition of surplus stock
    4,000 - Vendor quality surveys
    30,000 - Rework
    The total of the *quality* costs is:
    a. $619,000
    b. *$574,000*
    c. $615,000
    d. $570,000

75. In the previous problem, the total failure cost is:
    a. *$550,000*
    b. $30,000
    c. $350,000
    d. $380,000

76. In analyzing the cost data in question 74, we can conclude that
    a. *Prevention cost is too low a proportion of total quality cost.*
    b. Total of the quality costs is excessive.
    c. Internal failure costs can be decreased.
    d. Appraisal costs should be increased.

77. The design function which assigns probability of failures between components or subsystems is called:
    a. *Apportionment.*
    b. Significance.
    c. Confidence.
    d. Qualification.

78. An important aid to the quality supervisor in the area of record keeping and data processing is:
    a. Adaptability of records to computer processing.
    b. *Using well-designed forms and records.*
    c. Getting sufficient copies of records and reports distributed to key personnel.
    d. Training inspectors to follow inspection instructions and procedures.

79. What piece of data processing equipment can facilitate the handling of common quality control calculations on EDP equipment?
    a. Boolean algebra translator.
    b. *Collator.*
    c. Matrix inverter.
    d. Tensor analyzer.

80. Tabular arrays of data and graphs on the same page are especially useful in quality control work because:
    a. Both are there for those who don't like graphs only.
    b. Graphs help spot data transposition or errors.
    c. Control limits can be easily applied.
    d. *All of above.*

81. For complex electronic equipments, the major contributor to repair time is generally:
    a. *Diagnosis.*
    b. Disassembly/reassembly.
    c. Remove/replace.
    d. Final checkout.

82. What is the major drawback to using punch cards in a sophisticated information retrieval system?
    a. They answer only one question in a complete pass of the file.
    b. They do not store sufficient information.
    c. They take up too much space.
    d. *They are not as fast as magnetic tape.*

83. The sequence of punched fields for punched cards generally should be the same as:
    a. The data from previous reports with similar source data.
    b. Prescribed from the output report.
    c. No generally accepted practice can be prescribed.
    d. *The data to be punched from the original documents.*

84. A reliability test conducted during the pre-production stage is called:
    a. Demonstration test.
    b. Acceptance test.
    c. Significance test.
    d. *Qualification test.*

85. How many standard deviation units, symmetrical about the mean, will span an area around the mean of 40 percent of the total area under the normal curve?
    a. ±0.84
    b. *±0.52*
    c. ±1.28
    d. -0.25

86. A process is checked at random by inspection of samples of four shafts after a polishing operation, and $\bar{X}$ and R charts are maintained. A person making a spot check measures two shafts accurately, and plots their range on the R chart. The point falls just outside the control limit. He advises the department foreman to stop the process. This decision indicates that:
    a. The process level is out of control.
    b. The process level is out of control but not the dispersion.
    c. The person is misusing the chart.
    d. *The process dispersion is out of control.*

87. If X and Y are dependent random variables, and if X has variance 4 and Y has variance 3, then the variance of 5X - Y is:
    a. 103
    b. 23
    c. 17
    d. *Unknown.*

88. Test and inspection equipment should be:
    a. Replaced periodically.
    b. Covered when not in use.
    c. *Calibrated periodically.*
    d. As sophisticated as possible.

89. A process is in control with $\bar{p}$ = 0.10 and n = 100. The three-sigma limits of the np-control chart are:
    a. *1 and 19*
    b. 9.1 and 10.9
    c. 0.01 and 0.19
    d. 0.07 and 0.13

90. The metric system:
    a. Is based upon the circumference of the earth's equator.
    b. Originated in England.
    c. Is better than the inch-pound system.
    d. *Is legal in the United States.*

THEORY

1. Accuracy is:
   a. Getting consistent results repeatedly.
   b. Reading to four decimals.
   c. Using the best measuring device available.
   d. Getting an unbiased true value.
2. Classification of characteristics:
   a. Is the same as classification of defects.
   b. Can only be performed after product is produced.
   c. Must have tolerances associated with it.
   d. Is independent of defects.
3. In planning EDP applications, which element is necessary to reduce computing costs:
   a. Selecting quality control applications having little input and output but extensive calculations.
   b. Selecting applications with high volume input and output but simple calculations.
   c. A limited number of highly repetitive jobs.
   d. A group of jobs where output of one determines the input of another.
4. A Latin square design is an experimental design which:
   a. Cannot be used when an estimation of the interaction effects is desired.
   b. Affords a good estimate of interaction effects.
   c. Is useful because the underlying distributions need not be normal.
   d. Avoids the need to assume that the effects are additive.
5. Measurement error:
   a. Is the fault of the inspector.
   b. Can be determined.
   c. Is usually of no consequence.
   d. Can be eliminated by frequent calibrations of the measuring device.
6. Precision is:
   a. Getting consistent results repeatedly.
   b. Reading to four or more decimals.
   c. Distinguishing small deviations from the standard value.
   d. Extreme care in the analysis of data.
7. The concept of accelerated cycling or burn-in program of all devices for six months under normal operating conditions would:
   a. Reduce premature failures in use.
   b. Improve constant failure rate probability.
   c. Be of little use.
   d. Assure an acceptable quality to the customer.
8. In the failure rate model shown below, the part of the curve identified as A represents:

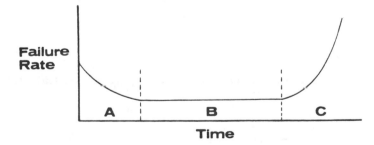

   a. The "bath tub" curve.
   b. Random and independent failures fitting a Poisson model
   c. The debugging period for complex equipment.
   d. The wear-out period.
9. What results can you expect from QIE in the area of quality costs?
   a. Lowered equipment utilization factors.
   b. Reduced percents defective for both scrap and rework.
   c. Less extensive and complicated equipment maintenance.
   d. Decreased quality control direct and indirect labor.
10. The most effective tool for action in any quality control program is:
   a. The effect on profits.
   b. The type and scope of quality reporting.

---

   c. The dynamic nature of the quality manager.
   d. Valid feedback.
11. The application of human factors in a plant production environment:
   a. Identifies reasons why errors are made.
   b. Is a practical example of using psychological techniques on workers.
   c. Is identified with a formal quality motivation program.
   d. Relates attitudes and prejudices among plant personnel.
12. A goal of quality cost report should be to:
   a. Get the best product quality possible.
   b. Be able to satisfy MIL-Q-9858A.
   c. Integrate two financial reporting techniques.
   d. Indicate areas of excessive costs.
13. The concept of quality cost budgeting:
   a. Involves budgeting the individual elements.
   b. Replaces the traditional profit and loss statement.
   c. Does not consider total quality costs.
   d. Considers the four categories of quality costs and their general trends.
14. When a new manufacturing process is contemplated, an important reason for scheduling a trial production lot is:
   a. To prove engineering feasibility.
   b. To prove that the pilot plant results are the same as those in the production shop.
   c. To prove that the tools and processes can produce the product successfully with economic yields.
   d. That it is inexpensive.
15. The effective supervisor:
   a. Sees his role primarily as one of making people happy.
   b. Sometimes does a job himself because he can do it better than others.
   c. Has objectives of growth and increased profit by working through other people.
   d. Assumes the functions of planning, decision making and monitoring performance, but leaves personnel development to the personnel department.
16. Sources of quality cost data do not normally include:
   a. Scrap reports.
   b. Labor reports.
   c. Salary budget reports.
   d. Capital expenditure reports.
17. To achieve consistent lot-by-lot protection the receiving inspector should:
   a. Allow no defective product into the shop.
   b. Return all rejected lots to the vendor.
   c. Not know how the vendor inspects the product.
   d. Use a sampling plan based on LTPD.
18. Which one of the following would most closely describe machine process capability?
   a. The process variation.
   b. The total variation over a shift.
   c. The total variation of all cavities of a mold, cavities of a die cast machine or spindles of an automatic assembly machine.
   d. The variation in a very short run of consecutively produced parts.
19. A correlation problem:
   a. Is solved by estimating the value of the dependent variable for various values of the independent variable.
   b. Considers the joint variation of two measurements, neither of which is restricted by the experimenter.
   c. Is the one case where the underlying distributions must be geometric.
   d. Is solved by assuming that the variables are normally and independently distributed with mean = 0 and variance = σ_e^2
20. The ratio: $\dfrac{\text{probability density function}(t)}{\text{reliability}(t)}$ is called:
   a. Useful life.
   b. Failure rate.
   c. MTBF
   d. Median.
21. For the exponential model, the reliability at mean time to failure is about:
   a. 37%
   b. 50%

c. 67%
d. 73%

22. A "p" chart:
   a. Can be used for only one type of defect per chart.
   b. Plots the number of defects in a sample.
   c. *Plots either the fraction or percent defective in order of time.*
   d. Plots variations in dimensions.

23. "Maintainability" is:
   a. The probability that a system will not fail.
   b. The process by which a system is restored to operation after failure.
   c. *A characteristic of design and installation.*
   d. The time required to restore a system to operation after failure.

24. The basic reason for randomness in sampling is to:
   a. Make certain that the sample represents the population.
   b. *Eliminate personal bias.*
   c. Guarantee to reduce the cost of inspection.
   d. Guarantee correct lot inferences.

25. To state that the levels of a factor are fixed indicates that:
   a. *The levels are to be set at certain fixed values.*
   b. The equipment from which the data are collected must not be moved.
   c. The factors under consideration are qualitative.
   d. The levels were chosen from a finite population.

26. When considering qualitative and quantitative factors in the same designed experiment:
   a. *The sum of squares for the qualitative factors can still be calculated even though no numerical scale can be attached to the levels.*
   b. Tables of orthogonal polynomials do not apply because no numerical scale can be attached to one of the factors.
   c. The interactions between qualitative and quantitative factors no longer make sense.
   d. The tables of orthogonal polynomials apply to both types of factors if the levels of each are equally spaced.

27. Quality information equipment (QIE) is the physical apparatus which is concerned with:
   a. Data collection and analysis.
   b. Data collection, storage and retrieval.
   c. Data collection and storage.
   d. *Data collection, analysis and feedback.*

28. When constructing a factorial experiment, one of the following is true:
   a. Factorial experiments may not contain any number of levels per factor. They must be the same for each factor.
   b. *Confounding takes place in factorials when we run a fractional part of the complete experiment.*
   c. Contrasts and treatment combinations are the same.
   d. In factorials, the factors must be quantitative.

29. Characteristics are often classified (critical, major, etc.) so that:
   a. Equal emphasis can be placed on each characteristic.
   b. Punitive action against the responsible individuals can be equitably distributed.
   c. *An assessment of quality can be made.*
   d. A quality audit is compatible with management desires.

30. True testing variability can be obtained in a destructive testing situation under one of these conditions:
   a. Enough samples have been tested.
   b. *It cannot be obtained.*
   c. All samples are taken closely together.
   d. The same person and instrument are used.

31. Recognizing the nature of process variability, the process capability target is usually:
   a. Looser than product specifications.
   b. The same as product specifications.
   c. *Tighter than product specifications.*
   d. Not related to product specifications.

32. There are two basic aspects of product quality:
   a. In-process and finished product quality.
   b. Appraisal costs and failure costs.
   c. *Quality of design and quality of conformance.*
   d. Impact of machines and impact of men.

33. The error term ϵ_{ij} of the population model $X_{ij} = \mu + \tau_{ij} + \epsilon_{ij}$ is usually considered:
   a. Normally and independently distributed with mean = 0, variance = 1.
   b. Normally and randomly distributed with mean = 0, variance = 1.
   c. Randomly distributed with mean = 0, variance = σ_e^2

d. *Normally and independently distributed with mean = 0, variance = σ_e^2.*

34. A random variable:
   a. *May be either discrete or continuous.*
   b. Is called "random" because it depends on the normal distribution.
   c. Is called "variable" because it refers to the variance.
   d. Is all of the above.

35. Which one of the following is a true statement of probability?
   a. P(E and F) = P(E) + P(F).
   b. P(E or F) = P(E)·P(E/F).
   c. *P(E or F) = P(E) + P(F) − P(E and F).*
   d. P(E and F) = P(E) + P(F) − P(E and F).

36. When finding a confidence interval for mean μ based on a sample size of n:
   a. Increasing n increases the interval.
   b. Having to use s_x instead of σ decreases the interval.
   c. The larger the interval, the better the estimate of μ.
   d. *Increasing n decreases the interval.*

37. A parameter is:
   a. A random variable.
   b. A sample value.
   c. *A population value.*
   d. The solution to a statistical problem

38. Which trigonometric function finds the most use in ordinary angular measurement?
   a. *Sine.*
   b. Cosine.
   c. Tangent.
   d. Cotangent.

39. In the pre-production phase of quality planning, an appropriate activity would be to:
   a. Determine responsibility for process control.
   b. *Determine the technical depth of available manpower.*
   c. Establish compatible approaches for accumulation of process data.
   d. Conduct process capability studies to measure process expectations.

40. Process acceptance involves decision making with regard to:
   a. The type of equipment or machinery used to process items during manufacture.
   b. *Items not yet made; that is, approval of "first piece" and periodic checks during a production run.*
   c. Items already made regardless of the technique used to control quality during processing.
   d. Acceptance sampling using MIL-STD-105D.

41. The control chart that is most sensitive to variations in a measurement is:
   a. p chart.
   b. pn chart.
   c. c chart.
   d. *$\bar{X}$ and R chart.*

42. When one first analyzes quality cost data, he might expect to find that, relative to total quality costs:
   a. Costs of prevention are high.
   b. Costs of appraisal are high.
   c. *Costs of failure are high.*
   d. All of above.

43. The assumed probability distribution for the control chart for number of defects is the:
   a. Binomial distribution.
   b. *Poisson distribution.*
   c. Normal distribution.
   d. Student's "t" distribution.

44. A statistic is:
   a. The solution to a problem.
   b. A population value.
   c. A positive number between 0 and 1 inclusive.
   d. *A sample value.*

45. Sensitivity is:
   a. Extreme care in data analysis.
   b. *Ability to distinguish differences in the response variable.*
   c. Getting the true result.
   d. Using the best measuring device.

46. Quality costs should *not* be reported against which one of the following measurement bases:
   a. Direct labor.
   b. Sales.
   c. *Net profit.*
   d. Unit volume of production.

47. A computer "program" is:
    a. The overall computer project for an entire company.
    b. *A set of instructions to accomplish a given set of calculations.*
    c. A subset of instructions later patched into a larger project
    d. Instructions written only in basic computer language

48. A 3² experiment indicates:
    a. Two levels of three factors.
    b. Three independent variables and two dependent variables.
    c. *Three levels of two factors.*
    d. Two go-no-go variables and three continuous variables.

49. Information generated in a designed experiment:
    a. Always results in an analysis of variance table.
    b. Is based on the fact that "the variance of the sum is the sum of the variances."
    c. Must always be quantitative.
    d. *May be based on values which are not necessarily numerical.*

50. Historically, under the sorting-inspection type of quality control function:
    a. When failure costs rise, appraisal costs fall.
    b. *Failure and appraisal quality costs trend together.*
    c. When failure costs fall, appraisal costs rise.
    d. Failure and appraisal costs generally remain unchanged.

51. A classification of characteristics makes it possible to:
    a. Separate the "vital few" from the "trivial many" kinds of defects.
    b. *Direct the greatest inspection effort to the most important quality characteristics.*
    c. Establish inspection tolerances.
    d. Allow the inspector to choose what to inspect and what not to inspect.

52. A frequency polygon:
    a. *Is a plot of connected points whose ordinates are proportional to cell frequencies.*
    b. Is also known as a cumulative relative frequency graph.
    c. Is also known as a sample distribution function.
    d. Applies only to discrete random variables.

53. The beta risk is the risk of:
    a. Selecting the wrong hypothesis.
    b. *Accepting an hypothesis when it is false.*
    c. Accepting an hypothesis when it is true.
    d. Rejecting an hypothesis when it is true.

54. If two-sigma limits are substituted for conventional three-sigma limits on a control chart, one of the following occurs:
    a. Decrease in alpha risk.
    b. Increase in beta risk.
    c. *Increase in alpha risk.*
    d. Increase in sample size.

55. What conditions are now developing which *require* the installation of QIE for continued quality control effectiveness?
    a. Need for better vendor-vendee relations.
    b. *Mechanization and automation of manufacturing operations.*
    c. Automation and mechanization of data processing activities.
    d. New and more accurate measurement methods.

56. The hypergeometric distribution is:
    a. *Used to describe sampling without replacement from a finite population where there are several outcomes for each trial.*
    b. A continuous distribution.
    c. A discrete distribution with its expected value equal to its variance
    d. The limiting distribution of the sum of several independent discrete random variables.

57. The two factors that have the most to do with determining an attributes sampling plan (assuming a binomial distribution) are:
    a. *Sample size and rejection number.*
    b. Lot size and sample size.
    c. Lot size and acceptance number.
    d. None of above.

58. Ratios of two variances drawn from the same normal population are described by which one of the following distributions?
    a. *F.*
    b. Student's "t".
    c. Chi-square.
    d. Normal.

59. Defining the required data output should be:
    a. Performed next after the use of a computer is economically justified.
    b. Performed next after input preparation.
    c. Done in such a way as to optimize computing formulas.
    d. *The first step in computer planning.*

60. Quality cost trend analysis is facilitated by comparing quality costs to:
    a. Manufacturing costs over the same time period.
    b. *Appropriate measurement bases.*
    c. Cash flow reports.
    d. QC department budget.

61. 100 percent inspection is:
    a. *Used to sort items.*
    b. At best only 60 percent effective.
    c. Assures a satisfactory outgoing quality level.
    d. Is theoretically unsound but is an excellent practice.

62. The basic statistical principle in EVOP is the:
    a. *Ability to find small significant differences through large sample sizes.*
    b. Operating with low levels of confidence.
    c. Making large changes in independent variables.
    d. None of these.

63. The following is an example of what type of response surface?

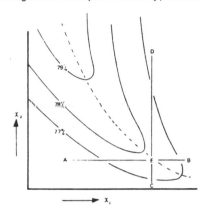

    a. *Rising ridge.*
    b. Maximum or minimum
    c. Stationary ridge.
    d. Minimax.

64. When considering a factorial experiment, observe that:
    a. This experiment cannot be used when complete randomization is necessary.
    b. *A main effect may be confounded.*
    c. This type of design is not encountered often in industrial experiments.
    d. One of the advantages is that an exact test always exists for all effects.

65. The factor D_4 used in $\overline{X}$ and R control charts is:
    a. *The distance between the mean and the upper control limit of a range chart.*
    b. The number of defects in a second sample.
    c. The constant which corrects the bias in estimating the population standard deviation from the average range of randomly drawn samples.
    d. The probability that $\overline{X}$ is in control.

66. The power of efficiency in designed experiments lies in the:
    a. Random order of performance.
    b. The sequential and cyclical procedure of conjecture to design to analysis and back to conjecture.
    c. *Hidden replication.*
    d. The large number of possible combinations of factors.

67. In planning process controls:
    a. Deciding whether the process runs or not is determined by whether the resulting product conforms or not.
    b. *The basic approach follows the servomechanism cycle so common in engineering.*
    c. Collection of information goes hand-in-hand with decision-making.
    d. Meeting process specification tolerances is the same as meeting product tolerances.

68. In the planning for quality information equipment, an appropriate activity would be to:
    a. Review present process capabilities to permit correlation with newer processes.
    b. *Establish training plans as required for the operation of the equipment.*
    c. Establish the routine for checkout and calibration tooling.
    d. Evaluate process cost relative to performance.

69. The most important reason for a checklist in a process control audit is to:

a. Assure that the auditor is qualified.
b. Minimize the time required for audit.
c. Obtain relatively uniform audits.
d. Notify the audited function prior to audit.

70. In the analysis of variance:
a. The total sum of squares of deviations from the grand mean is equal to the sum of squares of deviations between treatment means and the grand mean minus the sum of squares of deviations within treatments.
b. The total standard deviation is equal to the sum of the standard deviation for the treatment effect plus the standard deviation of the random error.
c. The degrees of freedom are additive.
d. A basic population model can be constructed to represent the behavior of the experimentation.

71. It has been found that the more complex the inspection task, the less accurate the inspection becomes. This can be partially overcome by:
a. Using several inspectors in a team approach.
b. Reducing the inspection task to a scanning operation.
c. Providing inspectors with an unlimited amount of inspection time.
d. Restricting inspection time in order to encourage increased concentration on the part of the inspector.

72. In linear measurement, what overriding consideration should guide the quality control engineer in specifying the measuring instrument to be used?
a. The ability of the instrument to be read to one decimal place beyond the places in the base dimension or tolerance.
b. The ability of the instrument to meet an error design goal of 10 percent.
c. The combination of base dimension and tolerance as they relate to measurement error.
d. The ability of the instrument-inspector system to obtain the necessary correct information at minimum overall cost.

73. Double sampling is better than single sampling because:
a. It involves less inspection regardless of lot quality.
b. If the first sample rejects the lot the second sample will accept it.
c. It is more economical except when lots are of borderline quality.
d. It is easier to administer.

74. In every experiment there is experimental error. Which one of the following statements is true?
a. This error is due to lack of uniformity of the material used in the experiment and to inherent variability in the experimental technique.
b. This error can be changed statistically by increasing the degrees of freedom.
c. The error can be reduced only by improving the material.
d. In a well-designed experiment there is no interaction effect.

75. The intentional difference in the sizes of mating parts is the:
a. Specification.
b. Clearance.
c. Natural tolerance.
d. Satisfactory functioning.

76. The ultimate standard for U.S. units of measurement, used to verify all masters, is:
a. The official meter.
b. The imperial yard.
c. The length of a light wave.
d. The Geiger counter.

77. The primary visual consideration in designing an inspection workspace is:
a. The environmental color decor because of its psychological effect.
b. The size and shape of the inspection table or bench.
c. The illumination and how it is provided.
d. The traffic flow in or near the inspection station.

78. Let X be any random variable with mean μ and standard deviation σ. Take a random sample of size n. As n increases and as a result of the Central Limit Theorem:
a. The distribution of the sum $S_n = X_1 + X_2 + \ldots + X_n$ approaches a normal distribution with mean μ and standard deviation $\sigma/\sqrt{n}$.
b. The distribution of $S_n = X_1 + X_2 + \ldots + X_n$ approaches a normal distribution with mean μ and standard deviation $\sigma/\sqrt{n}$.
c. The distribution of X approaches a normal distribution with mean $n\mu$ and standard deviation $\sigma\sqrt{n}$.
d. None of the above.

79. In the regression equation y = mx + b, y increases with x in all cases:
a. If b is positive.
b. If b is negative.
c. If m is positive.
d. If m is negative.

80. The basic objective of a quality cost program is to:
a. Identify the source of quality failures.
b. Determine quality control department responsibilities.
c. Utilize accounting department reports.
d. Improve the profit posture of your company.

81. Management is constantly seeking new ways to make profitable use of their expensive computers. Which of the following computer applications promises to be the most beneficial from management's standpoint?
a. Decision making help in combination with simulation techniques.
b. Wider use as an accounting machine.
c. High density information storage and rapid retrieval rates.
d. Solution of complex mathematical formulas.

82. In comparing the philosophies of "tight tolerances loosely enforced" and "realistic tolerances rigidly enforced," we can conclude that:
a. The first one is preferred.
b. The second one is preferred.
c. Neither is really practical.
d. Both have a place in any production operation

83. Good forms design and layout are essential in both manual and electronic data processing because:
a. They are easier to read, check data, use and file.
b. They are cheaper (faster) to use although initial cost is higher than quickly made forms.
c. They help to avoid typographical errors.
d. All of above.

84. Random selection of a sample:
a. Theoretically means that each item in the lot had an equal chance to be selected in the sample.
b. Assures that the sample average will equal the population average.
c. Means that a table of random numbers was used to dictate the selection.
d. Is a meaningless theoretical requirement.

85. The binomial distribution is a discrete distribution and may be used to describe:
a. Sampling without replacement from a finite population.
b. The case of n independent trials with probabilities constant from trial to trial.
c. The case of n independent trials with several outcomes for each trial.
d. Sampling without replacement from a finite population where there are several outcomes for each trial.

86. One defective is:
a. An item that is unacceptable to the inspector.
b. The same as one defect.
c. A characteristic that may be unacceptable for more than one reason.
d. An item that fails to meet quality standards and specifications.

87. The permissible variation in a dimension is the:
a. Clearance.
b. Allowance.
c. Tolerance.
d. Measurement.

88. This expression $\dfrac{n!}{x!\,(n-x)!}\,p'^x(1-p')^{n-x}$ is the following:

a. General term for the Poisson distribution.
b. General term for the Pascal distribution.
c. General term for the binomial distribution.
d. General term for the hypergeometric distribution.

89. The standard deviation as a percent of the mean is called:
a. Relative precision.
b. Coefficient of variability.
c. Standard deviation of the mean.
d. Standard error.

90. Monte Carlo method refers to a technique for:
a. The simulation of operations when random variations are an essential consideration.
b. Programing roulette for maximum return.
c. Random sampling from homogeneous population.
d. Establishing quantitative values to unknown restrictive variables in linear programing.

CQE EXAMINATION STUDY GUIDE

OUTLOOK

Thomas Pyzdek, CQE

CQE Examination Study Guide

Outlook

Thomas Pyzdek, CQE

The body of knowledge of quality engineering has been growing explosively in the past decade. Sooner or later these changes will be reflected in new questions in the CQE examination. The *Outlook* is an attempt to anticipate possible new CQE examination questions. These are not official questions, of course. They are merely hypothetical. However, they are based on over fifteen years of experience with the CQE examination as a CQE, an instructor, an author and a proctor. Besides, the specific question asked should be immaterial to someone with a firm command of the subject matter.

As with the rest of the CQE Examination Study Guide, this *Outlook* should not be thought of as a stand-alone program of study. Rather, it is a guide to the vast body of knowledge which must be mastered if you want to pass the CQE examination. The references cited must be consulted if you don't have a firm grasp of the subject material.

The *Outlook* is organized as follows:

Part I   Representative questions as they might appear on a CQE examination.

Part II   References cited in Part I, listed alphabetically.

The typefaces used throughout the *Outlook* are

Question typeface

Choice typeface

Discussion typeface

The recommended approach to learning the material in the *Outlook* is

- ❑ Read and answer the question
- ❑ Check your answer immediately
- ❑ Read the explanation of the answer
- ❑ Consult the references for additional information

Possible questions

A sample of 100 bottles taken from a filler process produced the following: $\overline{X} = 11.95$ ounces, s = 0.01 ounces. The specifications for the filler are 12 ounces ±0.10 ounces. Based on these results you should

A. Do nothing because the specification limit is more than 3σ from the process mean.

B. Adjust the fill level back to the nominal value of 12 ounces.

C. Compute a confidence interval around the process mean and adjust the process if the nominal fill level is not in the confidence interval.

D. None of the above

The correct answer is **D**, none of the above. The problem with all of the answers is the method used to evaluate the process. The approach is simply wrong. Statistical process control methods are, by their nature, analytic statistical methods. The other class of statistical studies are enumerative studies. Deming (1950, 1966, chapter 7) and Deming (1953) describes enumerative statistical studies as those whose aim is to provide a basis for action on the contents

1

of the bowl regardless of the reasons why the bowl's contents are the way they are. An analytic statistical study is done to provide a basis for action to be taken on the cause system that produced the result. In other words, analytic studies must provide insight into why the result occurred. The method used here (computing $\overline{X}$ and s) provides no such insight and, thus, no basis for action on the process. Analytic methods such as time-series plots or control charts are needed. Figure 1 shows three different sets of data which could produce the observed results; the three situations result from different causes and require different action.

The problem of applying enumerative statistical methods to analytic situations is widespread. CQE's should know better.

A designed experiment was conducted on three new lathes being purchased for a machine shop which has seven similar lathes already in operation. The experiment showed, at a level of significance of $\alpha = 0.05$, that setting the feed rate to medium produced the best surface finish on the part. Based on these findings, and assuming no other important effects, the appropriate action is

A. Set all ten lathe speed settings to medium.

B. Set the speed settings of the three lathes in the experiment to medium.

C. Replicate the experiment until the significance level is 0.01 or better.

D. Attempt to determine why the results occurred before taking further action.

The correct choice is **D**. Choices B and C are incorrect because they suffer from the same difficulty discussed in the previous question; namely, they treat this analytical statistical situation as if it were enumerative. Choice A has a different problem, it demonstrates a failure to understand the concept of the frame.

Deming (1950, 1966, pp. 77-84) and Deming (1960, chapter 3) describes the frame as a means of access to the universe or to a sufficient portion thereof. Frames in the design of an experiment like this would be a list of the machines to be studied. The way this experiment was conducted only the new lathes were included in the frame, but choice A proposes applying the results to all lathes. The seven older machines are a different frame.

ISO 9000 is

A. A catalyst used in petroleum refining.

B. An international standard for acceptance sampling by attributes.

C. The name commonly used to describe a series of international standards and guidelines for quality systems.

D. The international equivalent to the Malcolm Baldrige National Quality Award.

ISO 9000 is a set of five standards for quality systems, choice **C**. The titles and ASQC equivalents are shown in the table below.

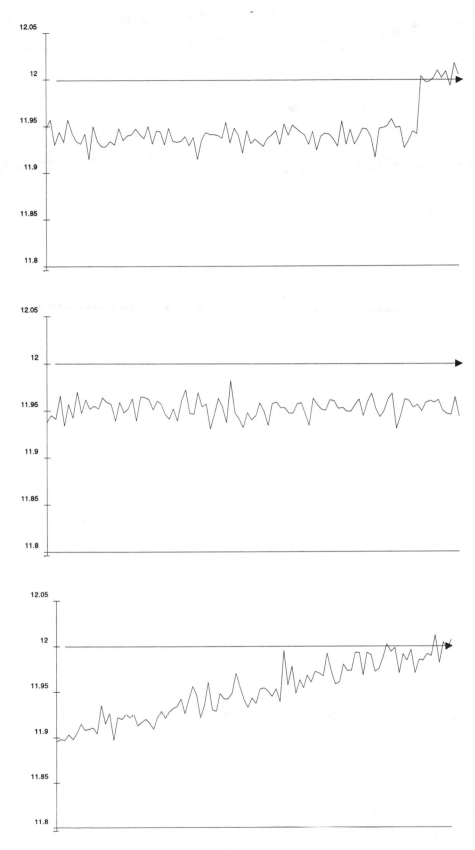

Figure 1-Different processes: one set of statistics

ISO Number	ASQC Equivalent	Title
ISO 9000	Q90	Quality management and quality assurance standards - guidelines for selection and use
ISO 9001	Q91	Quality systems - model for quality assurance in design/development, production, installation, and servicing
ISO 9002	Q92	Quality systems - model for quality assurance in production and installation
ISO 9003	Q93	Quality systems - model for quality assurance in final inspection and test
ISO 9004	Q94	quality management and quality system elements - guidelines

The guidelines in ISO 9000 are being adopted worldwide and they are being used to certify the quality systems of firms that wish to do business in EEC member states. Most Military contractors and suppliers to many commercial businesses will be required to demonstrate compliance to ISO 9000 requirements, usually through a registration/certification process. Different organizations throughout the world are authorized to conduct quality system assessments and to provide certification. In the US ASQC provides this service through their Registrar Accreditation Board.

The prospective CQE should study the standards themselves and the materials in Sawin and Hutchens (1991), Craig (1991), Puri (1991), Lofgren (1991) and Marquardt (1991).

The Malcolm Baldrige National Quality Award provides

A. A set of procedures designed to provide outstanding quality.

B. A list of requirements that, if met, will result in the certification of the company to provide goods and services to the federal government.

C. An award given by the Department of Defense to deserving suppliers for outstanding quality.

D. Recognition U.S. companies which excel in quality achievement and quality management.

The correct choice is **D**. The Malcolm Baldrige National Quality Award recognizes U.S. companies which have attained a high level of quality excellence and thereby competitive advantage in domestic and world marketplaces. Choice A is not correct because the Baldrige award is non-prescriptive. The prospective CQE should obtain a free copy of the current application guidelines from the National Institute of Standards and Technology at 1-301-975-2036; quantities are available from ASQC for a nominal price. The award process and strategies of some of the award winners is described in Pyzdek (1991). The award is not without its critics, an interesting discussion is presented in Crosby and Reimann (1991).

Total quality management (TQM) is

A. 100% inspection.

B. A method applied to critical items to assure their complete reliability.

C. The approach used by quality departments of suppliers to the department of defense.

D. None of the above

The correct choice is **D**. In a press release in June 1991, ASQC describes TQM as a customer-driven, process-improvement approach to management. The TQM committee of ASQC's Quality Management Division provides the following contrast of TQM and traditional management

Traditional	TQM
Bottom line emphasis	Quality orientation
Meet specifications	Continuous improvement
Get product out	Satisfy customer requirements
Short term focus	Long term mission
Delegated quality responsibility	Management led improvement
Defect detection	Defect prevention
People as cost burdens	People as assets
Independent work	Teamwork
Minimum cost suppliers	Quality partner suppliers
Departmentalized activities	Cross-functional team efforts
Management by edict	Employee empowerment
Sequential engineering	Simultaneous engineering
Gut-feel decisions	Data-driven decisions
Management by objectives	Management by planning

There have been dozens of books and hundreds of papers written on the subject of TQM. So many that ASQC Quality Press actually has a special advertising flier with TQM titles, and there are more titles introduced all of the time. For the prospective CQE seeking a succinct overview of the topic, I recommend the TQS series published by Quality magazine; TQS, which stands for total quality success, is equivalent to what I am calling TQM. During 1991 Quality magazine focused on TQS related topics in January, February, March, May, June, August, September, November and December. In particular, I recommend you read Bryce (1991, parts I and II).

Off-line quality control methods are a category of Taguchi methods which include:

A. Quality and cost control activities conducted at the product and process design stages to improve product manufacturability and reliability, and to reduce product development and lifetime costs.

B. Acceptance sampling at receiving inspection and in the supplier's plant.

C. Response surface methods based on process models designed to find optimal process settings.

D. Exploratory data analysis.

The correct answer is choice **A**. Taguchi methods are a controversial subject that, nevertheless, have been used successfully in quality applications in both the US and Japan. Although history has yet to determine exactly what will become of Taguchi methods in the distant future, it is almost certain that they will have some lasting impact on quality. The CQE candidate should be familiar with the basics of the Taguchi method including, at a minimum, the concepts of off-line and on-line quality control, the loss function, parameter design (including internal and external noise), tolerance design, orthogonal arrays and signal-to-noise ratios.

Taguchi methods have been the subject of almost as many books, articles and papers as TQM.

Pyzdek (1989) provides a survey of key Taguchi concepts. An excellent and concise overview of Taguchi methods is given by Kackar (1985). Kackar's paper, and Taguchi methods in general, are discussed by Box et al (1985). The best book on Taguchi methods that I've come across as an overall reference is Phadke (1989). Ross (1988, chapter 1) does an excellent job showing the application of the loss function. Unless you are a true Taguchi-ite, I don't recommend the two volume seminal work on the subject (Taguchi, 1987).

The house of quality is produced by which of the following methods?

A. TQM.

B. Quality function deployment.

C. Affinity diagrams.

D. ISO 9000.

The correct answer is **B**. Pyzdek (1991) describes quality function deployment (QFD) as a system for design of a product or service based on customer demands, a system that moves methodically from customer requirements to requirements for the products or services. King (1987) describes the QFD approach as consisting of four distinct phases:

Organization phase. Management selects the product or service to be improved, the appropriate interdepartmental team, and defines the focus of the QFD study.

Descriptive phase. The team defines the product or service from several different directions such as customer demands, functions, parts, reliability, cost, and so on.

Breakthrough phase. The team selects areas for improvement and finds ways to make them better through new technology, new concepts, better reliability, cost reduction, etc., and monitors the bottleneck process.

Implementation phase. The team defines the new product and how it will be manufactured.

QFD is a tool of TQM. It has been in use for many years and it will likely be around for years to come. One of the best compact presentations of the essentials, in my opinion, is Sullivan (1988). The same issue of Quality Progress contains several other good articles on QFD.

The interrelationship digraph, tree diagram and affinity diagram are examples of

A. The 7 M tools.

B. Classical SPC tools.

C. DOE techniques.

D. None of the above.

The three methods are a subset of what has come to be known as the 7 M tools, choice **A**. Pyzdek lists the following 7 M tools:

1. Affinity diagram.

2. Interrelationship digraph.

3. Tree diagram.

4. Matrix chart.

5. Matrix data analysis chart.

6. Process decision program chart (PDPC).

7. Arrow diagram.

Pyzdek (1991) also provides brief descriptions and examples of each of the 7 M tools. A more complete description is provided by Mizuno (1979).

The figure shown in figure 2 is interpreted as follows:

A. Customer satisfaction is determined solely by the quality of the product or service delivered.

B. Customer wants can be determined once and for all and used to design high quality products and services.

C. Customer wants, needs and expectations are dynamic and must be monitored continuously. Providing products or services that match the customer's expectations is not enough to assure customer satisfaction.

D. Customers will be satisfied if you supply them with products and services that meet their needs at a fair price.

Figure 2, the Kano Model, describes a situation of dynamic customer perceptions which are influenced by many factors, including the competition. Choice **C** is correct. Studies of customer satisfaction have demonstrated convincingly that customer satisfaction is not solely determined by the manufacturer's perception of the quality of the product or service; conformance to engineering requirements is an inadequate standard of quality. As figure 2 demonstrates, competitive pressure will make today's WOW features tomorrow's Must Have features. Customer expectations tend to increase steadily over time.

The Kano model is usually presented within the context of QFD. Kenny (1988) describes an application which uses the Kano model.

The search for industry best practices that lead to superior performance is called

A. Benchmarking.

B. Market research.

C. Total quality management.

D. Outsourcing.

The correct answer is **A**. Benchmarking was a key element of Xerox Corporation's strategy for recapturing lost markets through quality improvement, a strategy that led to their winning the Malcolm Baldrige National Quality Award in 1989. Benchmarking is covered in Camp (1989). An excellent article on benchmarking is Bemowski (1991).

To demonstrate compliance to a requirement that the C_{pk} index be at least 1.33 based on a $\pm 3\sigma$ spread, the quality engineer computed C_{pk} from fifty units selected at random from the production lot before it was delivered to the customer. Which of the following statements describes this approach to capability analysis.

A. It is invalid because no rational subgroup is used.

B. It is an acceptable method of computing C_{pk}.

C. It is invalid because the process may be out of control, which would not be detected with this approach.

D. It is invalid because the estimate of σ is not based on within-subgroup variation only.

E. All of the above except B.

The correct answer is **E**. Few methods have suffered from more abuse in recent years than capability analysis. Many large companies have

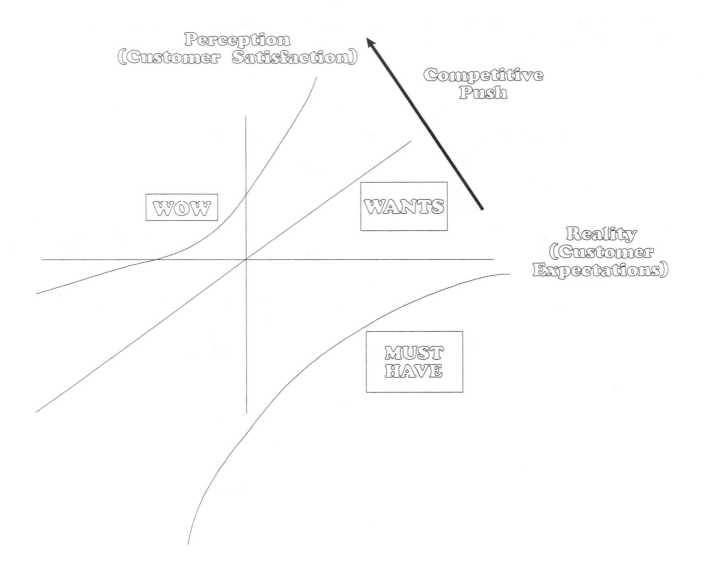

Figure 2-A model of customer satisfaction

mandated SPC, complete with capability analysis, of all key suppliers. The contractual requirements have been enforced at times by auditors who apparently don't have a good grasp of the underlying assumptions involved. The CQE should strive to understand all of the subtleties of capability analysis. Kane (1986) provides a technical overview of capability indices, including C_{pk}. Gunter (1989) gives an analysis of the shortcomings of C_{pk}. More recently, the C_{pm} index, sometimes called the Taguchi capability index, has been enjoying increased popularity. Like C_{pk}, the C_{pm} index accounts for both the process central tendency and its spread. However, C_{pm} works with a target value, while C_{pk} is based on the nearest tolerance limit. C_{pm} also has certain mathematical advantages over C_{pk}, such as a known probability distribution. The C_{pm} index is described in Chan, Cheng and Spiring (1988).

References Cited

Bemowski, K. (1991), "The benchmarking bandwagon," Quality Progress, January, pp. 19-24.

Box, G.E.P. et al (1985), "Discussion of off-line quality control, parameter design, and the Taguchi method," Journal of Quality Technology, Vol. 17, No. 4, pp. 191-209.

Bryce, G.R. (1991), "Quality management theories and their application," Quality, January, pp. 15-18 and February, pp. 23-26.

Camp, R.C. (1989), *Benchmarking*, copublished by ASQC Quality Press, Milwaukee, Wisconsin and Quality Resources, White Plains, New York.

Chan, L.K., Cheng, S.W. and Spiring, F.A. (1988), "A new measure of process capability: C_{pm}," Journal of Quality Technology, Vol. 20, No. 3, pp. 162-175.

Craig, R.J. (1991), "Road map to ISO 9000 registration," ASQC 45th Annual Quality Congress Transactions, pp. 926-930.

Deming, W.E. (1953), "On the distinction between enumerative and analytic surveys," Journal of the American Statistical Association, Vol 48, pp. 244-255.

Deming (1960), *Sample design in business research*, John Wiley & Sons, New York.

Deming, W.E. (Wiley, 1950; Dover, 1966), *Some theory of sampling*, Dover Publications Inc., New York.

Gunter, B.H. (1989), "The use and abuse of C_{pk}," a four part series presented in the Statistics Corner section of Quality Progress, Part 1: January; Part 2: March; Part 3: May; Part 4: July.

Kackar, R.N. (1985), "Off-line quality control, parameter design, and the Taguchi method," Journal of Quality Technology, Vol. 17, No. 4, pp. 176-190.

Kane, V.E. (1986), "Process capability indices," Journal of Quality Technology, Vol. 18, No. 1, pp 41-52. Corrigenda, vol. 18, no. 4, p. 265.

Kenny, A.A. (1988), "A new paradigm for quality assurance," Quality Progress, June, pp. 30-32.

King, Bob (1987), *Better designs in half the time: Implementing QFD in America*, Goal/QPC, Methuen, Mass..

Lofgren, G.Q. (1991), "Quality system registration, a guide to Q90/ISO 9000 series registration," Quality Progress, May, pp. 35-37.

Marquardt, D. et al (1991), "Vison 2000: the strategy for the ISO 9000 series standards in the '90s," Quality Progress, May, pp. 25-31.

Mizuno, S. ed. (1979), Management for quality improvement: the seven new QC tools, Productivity Press, Cambridge, Mass..

Phadke, M.S. (1989), *Quality engineering using robust design*, Prentice Hall, Englewood Cliffs, New Jersey.

Puri, S.C. (1991), "Deming + ISO 9000, a deadly combination for quality revolution," ASQC 45th Annual Quality Congress Transactions, pp. 938-943.

Pyzdek, T. (1988), *What every engineer should know about quality control*, Copublished by ASQC Quality Press, Milwaukee, Wisconsin and Marcel Dekker, Inc., New York.

Pyzdek, T. (1991), *What every manager should know about quality*, copublished by ASQC Quality Press, Milwaukee, WI and Marcel Dekker, New York.

Sawin, S.D. and Hutchens, S., Jr. (1991), "ISO 9000 in operation," ASQC 45th Annual Quality Congress Transactions, pp. 914-920.

Sullivan, L.P. (1988), "Policy management through quality function deployment," Quality Progress, June, pp. 18-20.

Taguchi, G. (1987), *System of experimental design: volumes one and two*, Copublished by Quality Resources, White Plains New York and American Supplier Institute, Dearborn, Michigan.

INDEX

A

acceptable quality level, see AQL
acceptance sampling, 12,15,18,23,
  41,80,95
accuracy, 106
alpha error, see type I error
analysis of variance, see ANOVA
ANOVA, 9,11,14,63,75,81,88
ansi y14.5, 36
AOQL, 11,23
AQL, 8,13,68-71,83
assignable cause, 18,93
ATI, 11
attributes sampling, 15,18,25,41,
  68-71
audit-quality, see quality audit
average outgoing quality limit,
  see AOQL
average total inspected, see ATI

B

beta error, see error-type II
binomial, 23,64,65,72,80

C

calibration, 33,105,110
capability-machine, 18,29
capability-process, 92
chi-square test, 85,90
classification of characteristics,
  97
classification of defects, 97
complaints, 54, 126
confidence interval, 81
contingency table, 82,90
contract, 26,102
control charts, 12,79,93
correlation coefficient, 62
cost-inspection, 99
cost-life cycle, 42
cost-quality, see quality cost
creep, 104

D

data analysis, 94,126
datum, 36
degrees of freedom, 82,90
dependent variable, 15
designed experiment, 13,16,19,22,
  90
dodge-romig tables, 11

E

elastic limit, 107
empty set, 17
error-measurement, 106
error-MS, 81
error-SS, 75
error-type I, 21
error-type II, 6
experiment-designed, see designed
  experiment
experiment-factorial, see factorial
  experiment
experiment-fractional factorial,
  see fractional factorial experiment
extrapolation, 15

F

F-test, 9
factor-fixed, 19
factor-random, 19
factorial experiment, 16,22
FDA, 34,102
feature control block, 36
field quality, 56,59
fixed factor, 19
food quality, 34,102,108
fractional factorial experiment,
  22

H

Hawthorne study, 57
holography, 35
hypergeometric, 12

I

independent variable, 15
inspection-100% vs. sampling, 95
inspection-accuracy, 40,127,128
inspection-error, 106
inspection-first piece, 29
inspection-incoming, see receiving
  inspection
inspection-instructions, 93
inspection-magnetic particle, 39
inspection-penetrant, 108
inspection-physical properties,
  35
inspection-procedure, 128
inspection-receiving, 31
inspection-reinspection, 103
inspection-ultrasonic, 109-110
inspector performance traits, 127

L

latin square, 16
life cycle cost, 42
linear regression, 15
lot tolerance percent defective,
  see LTPD
LTPD, 11

M

machine capability, 18,29,37
magnetic field, 36
magnetic particle inspection, 39
maintainability, 53
management, 58
material review board, see MRB
mean (see also x bar), 8,64,73,
  81,85
measurement standards, 105
median, 8
MIL-STD-105D, 8,13,68-71,83
MIL-STD-414, 68-71
mode, 8
model-regression, 15
motivation, 57,58-61
MRB, 99
multiple regression, 15
mutually exclusive events, 17

N

NDT, 35,39,108,109-110
negative specification, 34
non-conforming material, 28
non-destructive testing, see NDT
normal distribution, 7,8,29,73,76,
  85-87
null hypothesis, 6,14,19-21,88

O

OC curves, 12,14,25,78
operating characteristics curves,
  see OC curves
operational definition, 93
overflow, 55

P

p charts, 79
parameter, 6
penetrant inspection, 108
poisson, 22,64-65,72
policy, 33
population, 19-20
PRE-control, 96
precision, 106
privity of contract, 26
probability, 17,125
probability of acceptance, 8,64
procedure-written, 32
process capability, 7,92
product-integrity, 28
product-liability, 26,101
product-test, 34
profilometer, 38
program-quality control, 25

Q

quality assurance, 48
quality audit, 48-51,118-121
quality circles, 57
quality control program, 25
quality cost, 42-47,111-117
quality information systems, 54-55
quality function, 31
quality policy, 33

R

R, see range
random factor, 19
random variation, 18
range, 77
range charts, 12,77,87
regression, 15
reliability, 51-53,54,121-124,125
replication, 90

S

safety, 46
sampling-acceptance, see acceptance sampling
sampling-attributes, see attributes sampling
sampling-variables, see variables sampling
sigma, 10,20,66,85
software quality assurance, 53
specification-negative, 34
standard deviation, see sigma
standard error, 64
standards-measurement, 105
station control, 37
statistic, 6
statistical control, 92
supplier quality, 29,51,89
surface finish, 38

T

t-table, 81
terminal based linearity, 40
testing, 34
testing-electrical, 40
training programs, 127
type I error, 21
type II error, 6

U

ultrasonic inspection, 109-110
underflow, 55

V

variables sampling, 18,25,41, 68-71,78
variance, 11,85
variation-random, 18
vendor quality, see supplier quality

W

water break test, 104

X

x bar (see also mean) 10,64
x bar charts, 12,73,77,87

BOOK REVIEWS

Edited by Lawrence Leemis

Pyzdek, T., *What Every Engineer Should Know About Quality Control* .... John R. English   331

Berry, D. A., *Statistical Methodology in the Pharmaceutical Sciences* ...... Stephen J. Ruberg   331

Haaland, P. D., *Experimental Design in Biotechnology* .... Anita Thibeault   332

Barlow, R. J., *Statistics* .... Lloyd S. Nelson   333

Edosomwan, J. A., *Productivity and Quality Improvement* .... Satish J. Kamat   334

Doty, L. A., *Reliability for the Technologies* .... A. Clifford Cohen   334

What Every Engineer Should Know About Quality Control by *Thomas Pyzdek*. Marcel Dekker, New York, NY, and ASQC Quality Press, Milwaukee, WI, 1989. 251 pp. $49.75.

Reviewer: *John R. English*, Industrial Engineering Department, Texas A & M University, College Station, Texas 77843.

THE objectives of this book are to convey the fact that quality is a mixture of the subjective and the quantitative and to provide basic information on the essence of what quality control involves. These objectives are satisfied without the inclusion of the detailed descriptions and developments required to gain complete knowledge of the specific topics within quality control.

As established in the preface, the reader will learn of many important quality management and engineering methods. Upon completion of the reading of the text, an individual will have an elementary knowledge of the area of quality control and will be prepared to potentially identify any specific needs for quality control required in their present industrial environment. The author has included an excellent recommended reading list to support the specific needs of the reader.

The text is divided into twelve chapters. These chapters are Basic Concepts of Quality Control, Vendor Quality Assurance, Human Resources and Quality, Quality Organization and Management, Quality Information Systems, Probability and Statistics for Quality Control, Statistical Process Control, Acceptance Sampling, Designed Experiments and Taguchi Methods, Reliability, Measurement Error, and Japanese Approach to Quality Management. Clearly, each of these topics is of sufficient substance to justify a textbook on its own. Therefore, any effort to combine these into a single, introductory textbook is an admirable task, and to this end, the author has undertaken a difficult task.

The text describes management issues in Chapters 1 through 5 and 12. It may be necessary to supplement the text in some areas. For example, little discussion is provided concerning quality costs (which is reviewed in other texts, i.e. Pyzdek [1984]). Additionally, the text dedicates a complete chapter to the Japanese Approach to Quality Management, and within this discussion, there is little description of some modern methods (i.e., Quality Function Deployment).

In most cases, the overview of the quantitative methods (Chapters 6 through 10) are clear explanations of the objective of the methods encountered. For example, Chapter 9, Designed Experiments and Taguchi Methods, provides a clear overview of the methods encountered. But the details of these and the other quantitative methods presented in the text are often sketchy and sometimes confusing. While the text is appropriate for introductory training in quality control for engineers, it will serve an organization well to supplement this textbook with authoritative texts in each of the specific areas (i.e., statistical process control).

In summary, the text offers an excellent overview of modern qualitative and quantitative techniques within the area of quality control. Furthermore, it presents an introduction to the base of knowledge required for certification as a Quality Engineer (CQE) through the American Society for Quality Control (to supplement the preparation for the CQE, the author has written a study guide for the examination, Pyzdek [1984]). The book is well written and is easy to read. As would be expected, the presentation of the quantitative methods is excellent at the surface, but will require significant supplementary materials (for example, Pyzdek [1989]) if used within a technical training course.

References

Pyzdek, T. (1984). *CQE: Certified Quality Engineer Examination Study Guide*. Quality America, Tucson, AZ.

Pyzdek, T. (1989). *Pyzdek's Guide to SPC: Volume One/Fundamentals*. Quality America, Tucson, AZ and ASQC Quality Press, Milwaukee, WI.

Understand important quality management concepts and quality engineering methods and tools with . . .

WHAT EVERY ENGINEER SHOULD KNOW ABOUT
QUALITY CONTROL

A S Q C
Q
QUALITY
PRESS

(What Every Engineer Should Know Series/26)

CONSIDERATIONS OF QUALITY play a prominent role in all fields—particularly with recently focused attention on issues of consumerism, product and professional liability, and government regulation. American industries must improve quality if they are to remain competitive in world markets.

The engineering community occupies a vital function in the effort to advance quality—namely, that designs be well engineered for consistent reproduction.

Wading through the vast body of available information to form a compact, up-to-date treatment of the essentials of quality control, *What Every Engineer Should Know About Quality Control*

- **surveys significant features of quality control from the perspective of a practicing quality professional**—providing engineers with the fundamental elements of quality and how they work in actual practice

- **shows how to implement quality programs from beginning to end**—supplying practical, perceptive information for companies that seek to create their own quality programs

- **introduces statistical methods used in quality control and gives examples of how they are applied to quality control situations**—combining both theory and applications for a well-rounded, succinct look at the topic

- **discusses both technical and nontechnical aspects of quality control**—showing how quality control encompasses such diverse disciplines as mathematics, management, psychology, engineering, law, and human relations, all of which are necessary for success

Useful to both professionals and students, *What Every Engineer Should Know About Quality Control* contains drawings, equations, and tables, and is ideal reading for all engineers concerned with quality and product assurance, manufacturing and production managers, and upper-level undergraduate courses in industrial, civil, mechanical, electrical, and ceramic engineering.

THOMAS PYZDEK
Quality America, Inc.
Tucson, Arizona

October, 1988
272 pages, illustrated
$49.75 *(U.S. and Canada)*
$59.50 *(All other countries)*

CONTENTS

Basic Concepts of Quality Control
Vendor Quality Assurance
Human Resources and Quality
Quality Organization and Management
Quality Information Systems
Probability and Statistics for Quality Control
Statistical Process Control
Acceptance Sampling
Designed Experiments and Taguchi Methods
Reliability
Measurement Error
Japanese Approach to Quality Management
References and Recommended Reading
Appendix

ISBN: 0-8247-7966-5

Q
Quality Publishing, Inc.

Tucson, Arizona
800-628-0432

CQE Examination Study Guide

If you are preparing for the ASQC Certified Quality Engineer's examination, or if you are simply interested in developing a comprehensive understanding of Quality Engineering, you are faced with a formidable task. Quality Engineering is a vast field that encompasses many other disciplines. Until now the aspiring Quality Engineer had to find his own way through this mass of material, hoping that he allocated his time to the correct subjects.

The proof that this method was, at best, questionable is that nearly 50% of all who take the CQE examination fail. This fact bothered Thomas Pyzdek, who had taught CQE refresher classes for colleges and business clients in Arizona. It bothered him because he saw between 80% and 100% of his students pass the CQE examination on their first attempt. He knew that one reason was that the CQE refresher course helped these people focus their attention to the most

important topics. It disturbed him that many qualified CQE candidates were being unfairly deprived of their certification simply because they didn't have access to a qualified instructor.

His answer to this problem was the *CQE Examination Study Guide.* Pyzdek condensed all of his course materials into this book, including
- CQE refresher course outline, syllabus, and reading list.
- Multiple choice quizzes and answers.
- A final exam that simulates the real CQE exam.
- The ASQC certification program booklet.
- All previously published CQE exams.

In addition, the book includes **complete, detailed answers to all 170 questions in the CQE exam published in the July 1984 issue of** *Quality Progress* **magazine!** Along with the answers the book provides references for further study. The references go beyond just naming books.

It tells you which sections should be mastered. Also included are references to important articles in magazines or technical journals. In short, it's a lot like being in a CQE Refresher Class!

Order your copy of the CQE *Examination Study Guide* **today!**

#QAB002

What Every Manager Should Know About Quality

In today's business environment, and in tomorrow's, quality is a prerequisite for economic survival. This book provides the vital elements from the vast body of knowledge of quality control - offering managers a timely, accessible account of this important subject.

Supplying a thorough reading list that facilitates further investigation of a topic, this practical volume discusses underlying concepts of critically important quality techniques...covers the Taguchi approach in *nontechnical* terms...describes the mechan-

ics of the Malcolm Baldrige National Quality Award and strategies of past winners...details the Department of Defense's implementation of total quality management (TQM)...focuses on quality function deployment (QFD) and other modern tools of quality management...and more!

A valuable tool for both professionals and students, *What Every Manager Should Know About Quality* is a working reference for managers and supervisors in quality, manufacturing, engineering and purchasing; and managers of all types of service businesses.

1-800-628-0432
2405 N. Avenida Sorgo Tucson, Arizona 85749

Quantity Discounts   5–24: 5%   25–99: 10%   100+: 15%

30 day moneyback guarantee on all sales (freight charges not refunded). Shipping Charges:
$5 per order or actual freight charges, whichever is greater. Visa/MC/American Express accepted

 Quality Publishing, Inc.

PYZDEK'S Guide to SPC

About the Book

PYZDEK'S GUIDE TO SPC is written by Quality America's Founder and President, Thomas Pyzdek. It is co-published by Quality America and ASQC Quality Press. The book is part of a series based on materials used in ASQC seminars on SPC. Volume One, *Fundamentals*, provides information that everyone using SPC should know. Topics include organizing and implementing SPC; group dynamics; data collection; problem solving techniques (including cause & effect diagrams and flowcharts); Pareto analysis; histograms; scatter plots; run charts; x bar, R, and sigma charts; p, np, c, and u charts. The subject matter is presented in a text with an accompanying workbook to allow the reader to practice his or her new knowledge. Instructor's materials are also available. Included are 120 professionally prepared 2 color mylar overhead visuals in an attractive case. Also included is an Instructor's booklet with annotations for each overhead visual and a discussion of workbook exercises. These allow the instructor and the student the opportunity to fully explore each

topic. Later volumes in the series will include Volume Two, *Applications and Special Techniques* and Volume Three, *Advanced Topics.*

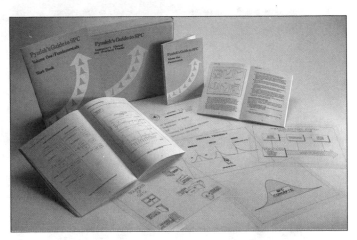

About the Author

Experience

For over 22 years Thomas Pyzdek has used SPC to improve quality and productivity for his employers and consulting clients, as well as in his own business operations. He's had hands-on experience with applications ranging from machine shops to chemical processes to service. This experience is evident on nearly every page of *Pyzdek's Guide to SPC*.

Teaching

Pyzdek taught his first class more than 15 years ago. Since then he has conducted hundreds of SPC seminars, both public seminars and on-site seminars, for thousands of students. Pyzdek has taught ASQC's course in SP/QC nationally for several years.

Writing

The author of the best-selling *An SPC Primer*, Pyzdek's writing style is famous for making difficult information easy to understand. Other books by Pyzdek include *The CQE Examination Study Guide* and *What Every Engineer Should Know About Quality Control*.

#QAB005   (Text)
#QAB006   (Workbook)
#QAB007   (Inst. Materials)

An SPC Primer *SPC Self-Teaching Guide*

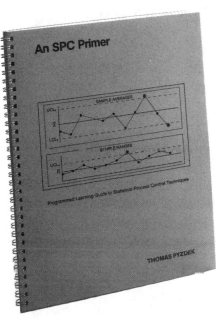

We learned that SPC need not be difficult to understand. In fact, we discovered, if the material is properly presented, SPC is so easy to understand it's simply amazing! The *SPC Primer* is a self-study book based on years of experience with the application and teaching of SPC. It is written in programmed learning format and it is designed to allow the reader to learn SPC at his or her own pace. Students begin with basic arithmetic and move ahead in small steps with constant feedback in the form of exercises. We've learned that SPC is not a spectator sport, and the *SPC Primer* makes sure that the student **knows** the material before allowing him to move ahead.

While the *SPC Primer* begins at a very elementary level, it doesn't insult the intelligence of the reader. There are no cartoons or cutesy drawings, just a complete description of all the major types of control charts. Charts described include X bar and R, moving range con-

trol charts for individuals, run charts, p charts, np charts, c charts and u charts. The book not only describes the construction of the charts, but their application as well. Also described are such important related topics as run tests, tests of normality, the central limit theorem and its importance in SPC, and process capability analysis. The Cp index is described in detail. An appendix with blank forms and worksheets is included.

Perhaps the most important evidence of the value of this book is the fact that it has been used by thousands of companies to train their employees. The book is in use by nearly every major firm in the United States, as well as many foreign countries. The *SPC Primer* is now in its eleventh printing, and still going strong. If you are looking for an introduction to SPC that is comprehensive but still easy to understand, this book is for you!

#QAB001

THOMAS PYZDEK

Thomas Pyzdek is President of Quality America, Inc., a leader in the growing field of quality improvement. His firm, based in Tucson, Arizona, publishes books and statistical process control (SPC) software used in over 19,000 firms around the world. In addition, he provides consulting and training services to clients worldwide.

Pyzdek is a frequent speaker at American Society for Quality Control (ASQC) Annual Quality Congresses and he teaches the national ASQC seminar in Statistical Process Quality Control. He has appeared as a speaker with Dr. W. Edwards Deming.

Pyzdek served on the Board of Examiners for the first Malcolm Baldrige National Quality Award. He attended the presentation of the first award by President Ronald Reagan at the White House.

Pyzdek is on the faculty of the University of Phoenix where he teaches TQM. He serves on the national ASQC TQM Committee, concerned with government TQM programs and the MB National Quality Award.

Pyzdek has written several popular books on quality, including *An SPC Primer, The CQE Examination Study Guide, Pyzdek's Guide to SPC*, and *What Every Engineer Should Know About Quality Control.* His next book, *What Every Manager Should Know About Quality Control* is scheduled for publication by marcel dekker, inc. in late 1990. He is senior editor of *The Quality Engineering Handbook.* His articles and papers have appeared in professional journals and magazines, such as Quality Engineering, Quality, and Quality Progress.

Quality America's SPC software, designed and developed by Pyzdek, is widely acknowledged as the easiest to use as well as the most powerful and reliable. His software sets the standard by which competing products are judged.

Over the years he has worked with many Fortune 500 firms, including General Motors, IBM, Avon Products, and Hughes Aircraft Company. He is an approved consultant in quality to Ford Motor Company and its suppliers. He was the technical consultant and a featured guest on a nationally marketed videotaped quality training program produced by Unisys Corporation. Pyzdek is frequently interviewed as a quality expert and he has done nationally televised satellite broadcasts on QFD and quality management.

Prior to founding his firm in 1983, Pyzdek was Head of Total Quality Assurance for Hughes Aircraft Company's Missile Systems Group. He joined Hughes in 1979 from Valmont Industries where he was Supervisor of Quality and Reliability Engineering. He earned a BS in Economics from the University of Nebraska in 1974, and an MS in Systems & Industrial Engineering from the University of Arizona in 1982 as the recipient of the prestigious Hughes Engineering Master's Fellowship. He is a senior member of the ASQC, an ASQC Certified Quality Engineer and an ASQC Certified Reliability Engineer.

Quality Publishing, Inc.

Tucson, Arizona
800-628-0432